W9-BEB-493

THE VICKSBURG CAMPAIGN

THE VICKSBURG CAMPAIGN

David G. Martin

GALLERY BOOKS
An Imprint of W. H. Smith Publishers Inc.
112 Madison Avenue
New York City 10016

Editorial development and design by Combined Books, Inc., 26 Summit Grove Avenue, Suite 207, Bryn Mawr, PA 19010.

Produced by Wieser and Wieser, Inc., 118 East 25th Street, New York, NY 10010.

This 1990 edition published by Gallery Books, an imprint of W.H. Smith, Publishers, Inc., 112 Madison Avenue, New York, NY 10016.

ISBN 0-8317-9127-6

CONTENTS

	Introduction	6
I.	**First Threats**	7
II.	**The Fall of New Orleans**	19
III.	**The Threats Become Real**	29
IV.	**The Saga of the *Arkansas***	39
V.	**Grant Takes Command**	47
VI.	**Grant the Relentless**	65
VII.	**Grant's Final Drive**	77
VIII.	**Vicksburg: The First Assaults**	111
IX.	**The Siege**	137
X.	**The Mine**	149
XI.	**The Surrender**	173
	Epilogue	180
	Bibliography	181

Introduction

Vicksburg, Mississippi, in 1860 was a thriving riverboat town with a population near 5,000, and the second largest city in the state. Situated atop the picturesque Walnut Hills on the eastern bank of the "Father of Waters," Vicksburg had docks that served the profitable local cotton plantations, which shipped their "white gold" to New Orleans, about 200 miles to the south. The city was also an important trading center, dealing with Natchez downstream and Memphis upstream, and with rail connections to the interior of Mississippi and Louisiana. Life for most of Vicksburg's citizens was leisurely and profitable, as it had been ever since the town was incorporated in 1825.

This serenity was shattered by the political events of early 1861. The state of Mississippi, heartened by South Carolina's secession three weeks earlier, voted on 9 January, 1861, to become the second state to leave the Union. Ironically, the citizens of Vicksburg had not been in favor of disunion—in the vote for convention delegates held on 7 January, Unionist candidates were elected over secessionists by a count of 561 to 175. The town nevertheless embraced the Southern cause, and was soon raising troops and placing cannons on its heights overlooking the river.

Little did Vicksburg's citizens realize that within a few months of secession their beloved town would become an armed camp, a fortress nicknamed the "Gibraltar of the West." Within two years the Mississippi River, source of Vicksburg's wealth and prosperity, would draw hordes of enemy troops to a great siege that was one of the most critical battle of the great Civil War. Here Union forces would attempt to wrest control of the river and so split the Confederacy in two, while the defenders of Vicksburg would fight to preserve the South's last link with the fertile grounds of the Trans-Mississippi. When Vicksburg finally fell on 4 July 1863—the same day Robert E. Lee's defeated Confederate army retreated from Gettysburg—the struggling Confederacy was dealt a mortal blow from which it could not recover.

The Vicksburg Campaign is more than the study of one of the greatest campaigns of the war. It is also a study in character, determination and perseverance. On one side, brave Confederate soldiers and generals strove to hold Vicksburg for two years against ever increasing odds with a heroism that has become famous in American popular history as beleaguered defenders who lived in caves, ate rats and mules, and printed their newspapers on wallpaper. On the other side, masterful Union strategy brought on the critical confrontation at Vicksburg, but this confrontation was not one with a preordained outcome. The eventual Union triumph was engineered by the determination of one man, Major General Ulysses S. Grant, victor at Fort Donelson and Shiloh, the man who spent seven months and risked his career attempting to crack Vicksburg. Once Vicksburg finally fell, Grant went on to equally great triumphs, at Chattanooga and Richmond, following a road that led ultimately to the White House. Had he failed to take Vicksburg, the later course of the war and all American history might well have been markedly different.

CHAPTER I

FIRST THREATS

When the Civil War began, Union Lieutenant General Winfield Scott, commander in chief of the armies, developed a quick and simple plan to crush the Confederacy: blockade its saltwater ports to cut off its foreign trade, and then take control of the Mississippi Valley to cut the Confederacy in two. Scott's plan was eagerly accepted by President Abraham Lincoln, who had grown up in the upper Mississippi basin and understood firsthand its commercial importance (Lincoln in his earlier years had worked for a time on the Ohio and the Mississippi, and had even once sailed past Vicksburg to New Orleans). When the first attack on New Orleans was being planned, Lincoln said to one of his admirals, "The Mississippi is the backbone of the Rebellion; it is the key to the whole situation. While the Confederates hold it, they can obtain supplies of all kinds, and it is a barrier against our forces."

Lincoln was most anxious for his forces to move quickly to seize the entire Mississippi line, especially Vicksburg. At a strategy meeting in early 1862 he stated, "It is not only necessary to have troops enough to hold New Orleans, but we must be able to proceed at once toward Vicksburg, which is the key to all that country watered by the Mississippi and its tributaries. If the Confederates once fortify the neighboring hills, they will be able to hold that point for an indefinite time, and it will require a large force to dislodge them. . . . I am acquainted with that region and know what I am talking about. We may take all the northern parts of the Confederacy and they can still defy us from Vicksburg. . . . see what a lot of land those fellows

In this contemporary photograph Vicksburg appears to be a peaceful and idyllic town. Later it was the sight of the most terrible siege of the Civil War.

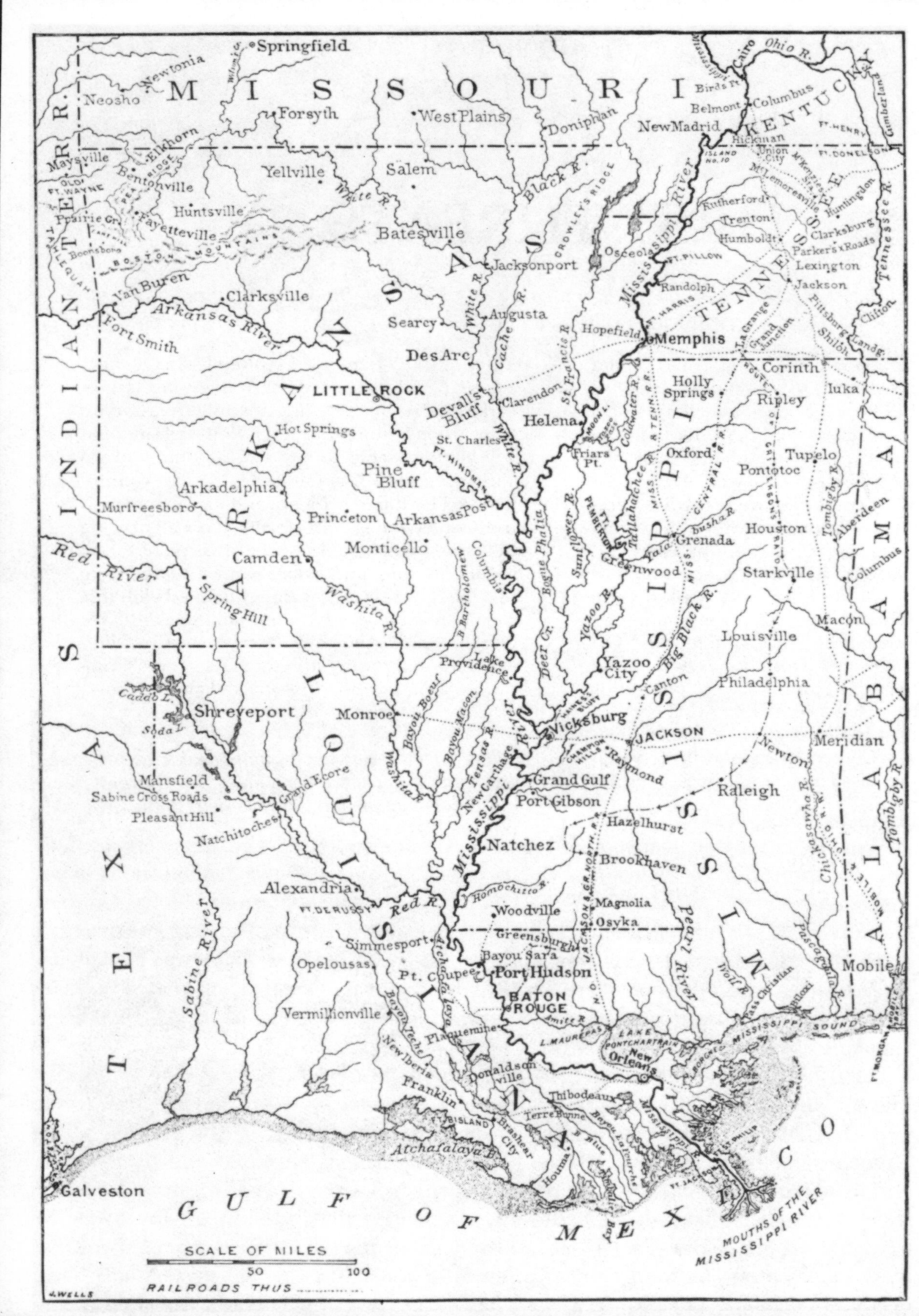

The Town of Vicksburg

The bluffs at Vicksburg had long been recognized as an important post on the Mississippi River. As early as the late 1500's, Spanish explorers had established a base named Fort Nogales on the Walnut Hills a little north of present day Vicksburg. The small fort was a minor trading center or over two hundred years, and certainly had no reason to grow as did New Orleans, some two hundred miles to the south. In fact, the fort was abandoned around 1800 and the future site of Vicksburg was left for wandering bands of Indians.

The modern story of Vicksburg begins in 1814, when the Walnut Hills were visited by a Methodist minister from North Carolina named Newet Vick. Vick saw the natural advantages of the site's physical location as well as its commercial potential for controlling north-south and east-west trade routes. So he set about laying out a town to be populated initially by his tribe of thirteen children and other assorted relatives he brought with him. Vick himself laid out the town's rectangular grid plan and chose the names of the streets, most of which were named for leading politicians of the day or tree species.

Newet Vick, the namesake of Vicksburg, was not fated to see his town grow and prosper. He died of yellow fever in an 1819 epidemic that also took away his wife. Leadership in building the town then fell to Vick's son-in-law., John Lane. By 1825 there were 150 souls residing there, enough to apply for a charter. Businessmen and professionals settled in the residential quarter, while the river front section became noted for its bordellos and gambling halls. The town, which was already off to a good start, grew even more in the 1830's when the newfangled steamboats increased river traffic dramatically and a railroad line was built to Jackson. Soon large cotton plantations were blossoming in the countryside nearby. Their owners used Vicksburg as their banking and commercial center, and even bought themselves spacious city homes to live in when not at their plantations. One of the most noted landowners near Vicksburg was Jefferson Davis, who had a plantation named "Brierfield" some twenty miles downriver.

In 1861 Vicksburg was a prosperous town of 5000 residents. It had plank sidewalks, the hospitals, four volunteer fire companies, five churches, a large public school and several private ones, and three daily newspapers. The town's most magnificent building was the Warren County Court House, located between Cherry and Monroe streets. It was an impressive building with pillars on each side and a cupola topped by a four sided German clock. Since the courthouse was located two hundred feet above the level of the river, the Union troops saw it clearly every day with its defiant Confederate flag flapping in the wind.

The objective, the "Gibraltar of the West."

hold, of which Vicksburg is the key. . . . The war can never be brought to a close until that key is in our pocket."

The citizens of Vicksburg, however, did not feel their town to be the object of any grand Yankee strategy. The war seemed too far away, in Charleston and Virginia and Kentucky. The new Confederacy's vast size and the length of the Mississippi seemed to isolate the town from the pending war. Nevertheless, the natives of Vicksburg patriotically set about raising troops to supplement their two companies of standing militia, the "Southrons" and the "Sharpshooters", known collectively as the "Vicksburg Battalion." The four new companies were christened, in the heady feelings of the day, "Warren County Guards," "Hill City Cadets," "Warren Dragoons," and "Vicksburg Light Artillery."

The first commander of the military post of Vicksburg was Captain J.F. Kerr, who was ordered by the state's governor "to take such position as would enable him to prevent any hostile expedition from descending the river." Kerr took three companies plus four cannons to the bluffs north of the city near the site of old Fort Nogalis. From there the defenders of Vicksburg fired their first hostile shots of the war on 11 January, 1861. Their object was a Northern steamboat, the *O.A. Tyler*, that was innocently carrying civilian trade goods from Cincinnati. A few shots from Kerr's guns sent the steamer scurrying north to the great cheers of the defenders.

The next few months were not as exciting in Vicksburg, except for a brief visit by Jefferson Davis in February when he was on his way to Montgomery, Alabama, to be inaugurated president of the Confederacy (Davis owned a plantation twenty miles south of Vicksburg). Since Vicksburg seemed to be under no military threat, her troops were siphoned off to far flung defenses at Pensacola, Montgomery, and Richmond. Only a bare guard remained in Vicksburg.

The town of Vicksburg felt secure in the event of an attack from the south because of the vaunted defenses of New Orleans. Consequently all attention was focused on Union activity to the North, and the few guns trained in that direction. The town indeed had reason to fear an attack from the north. Soon after Fort Sumter fell in April, Union Commander John Rodgers began what would become the Mississippi River Squadron when he purchased three steamboats for conversion to military use, the *Tyler*, *Lexington*, and *Conestoga*. These and additional boats were gathered at the important naval station located at Cairo, Illinois, where the Ohio River merged with the Mississippi.

One of the first Federal gunboats to prowl the Mississippi River, the Tyler.

The St. Louis, a vessel that saw action on the Mississippi from the battle of Columbus to Forts Henry and Donelson to Vicksburg.

This inland fleet came under the command of Admiral Andrew Foote on 6 September, 1861. Over the next four months, Foote's growing fleet was reinforced by seven specially designed and newly constructed warships known as the "city class" gunboats. Each of these was able to carry 13 cannons and was armed with two and one-half inches of armor plate (for more details of their construction, see the *USS Cairo*). The Confederates heard of the creation of this riverine fleet of gunboats and erected defenses to stop them at New Madrid, Missouri, Island No. 10, Tennessee, and especially at Columbus, Kentucky.

In conjunction with the naval forces gathered at Cairo, a small army detachment was gathered at the same point. Their commander as of late August was a little known Illinois West Pointer named Ulysses S. Grant. Grant was not one to sit still, and soon prepared to make a dash on the Confederate position at Belmont, Missouri, located opposite the strong fort at Columbus, Kentucky. His sudden attack on November 7 met initial success, but was beaten back when Confederate reinforcements arrived while many of his men were distracted pillaging a captured camp.

Grant formulated a bold new plan over the winter. Columbus was too strong a post to take by naval attack or direct land assault. On the other hand it was, he thought, vulnerable to a flanking movement that would cut it off from its supply bases in inland Kentucky and Tennessee. Grant felt the best way to get at Columbus was to move against two lesser known forts about 70 miles to the east, Fort Henry on the Tennessee River and Fort Donelson on the Cumberland River. Grant received the full backing and cooperation of Admiral Foote for such a campaign. Foote's fleet—consisting of 45 gunboats and 38 mortar boats— would escort Grant's transports and then provide firepower to help reduce the forts.

A man whose talent had yet to be recognized, Brigadier General U.S. Grant at the beginning of the Civil War.

Bloody carnage in Fort Henry after a 42-pound rifled gun explodes as Confederate defenders return fire from Foote's gunboats.

Grant's campaign against Forts Henry and Donelson was a masterful piece of strategy. Fort Henry fell to a naval bombardment on 6 February. Fort Donelson was captured ten days later after a sharp battle. Grant's twin victories broke the back of the Confederate defensive line in Tennessee. Nashville fell on the 23rd, and the important manufacturing area in central Tennessee soon followed suit.

Grant's success encouraged General Henry Halleck, the overall Union commander in the West, to send Brigadier General John Pope in a drive against Memphis, Tennessee's principal commercial center in the Mississippi. To get at Memphis, Pope had first to deal with Columbus and Island No. 10. Like Grant, Pope wisely chose not to attack Columbus head on. Instead, he moved against New Madrid, some thirty miles downstream from Columbus. This maneuver, connected with Grant's capture of Forts Henry and Donelson, completely isolated the Confederate fortress at Columbus, which was evacuated at the end of February without a shot being fired. Most of its 140 cannons were transferred south to Island No. 10, which became Pope's new objective.

While Pope advanced directly down the Mississippi toward Island No. 10, Grant moved up the Tennessee. By early March he reached Savannah, near the Mississippi River. Here he was ordered by his superior, General Halleck, to make camp and await the arrival of Don Carlos Buell's Army of the Ohio. Grant accordingly formed his troops loosely in a woods near a chapel called Shiloh. Here he was attacked by Confederate General A.S. Johnston on 6 April in one of the war's greatest battles. Johnston's surprise attack caught Grant completely unaware, but Confederate total victory was not achieved when Johnston fell in combat. Grant recovered on the next day, and aided by reinforcements from Buell's slowly arriving army, won the battle.

The Battle of Shiloh changed the complexion of the War in the West. Johnston had stripped most Confederate defenses in the area in order to form the force that attacked Grant. Now that the battle was lost, the Confederate West was wide open to further Union penetration. The Yankees, at first did not take advantage of the situation. Pope, who had captured Island No. 10 on 8 April after a three-week siege, was diverted from Memphis and ordered to join Halleck, Buell and Grant for a drive on Corinth, Mississippi. Despite an overwhelming superiority in strength, Halleck's advance on Corinth was so deliberate he did not capture the town until late May. He then paused to consider what to do next—advance west towards the Mississippi, south towards Montgomery, or east towards Chattanooga and Atlanta.

After Pope was ordered to join Halleck, the task of clearing the Mississippi reverted for awhile to the Union fleet, which did not at first fare well. On 10 May, five Yankee gunboats were suddenly attacked near Fort Pillow by the River Defense Fleet in a battle now called Plum Run Bend. Here the Confederates managed to sink the Union ships *Cincinnati* and *Mound City* in ram attacks, though their own boats suffered badly.

Grant's Yankees feverishly attempt to repel a Confederate assault under Albert Sidney Johnston on the first day of the Battle of Shiloh.

The Boys' War

Thousands of boys under the age of 18 fought on both sides during the Civil War. Exact records of enlistment ages were not kept by either side. However, two studies have shown that significant numbers of minors really did participate in the war. In 1866 members of the U.S. Sanitary Commission received records of 1,000,000 of the approximately 2,400,000 Union soldiers. They determined that 10,233 of these were below age 18, and of those, 773 were 15, 330 were 14, and 127 were 13 or younger (including 27 age 10 or under). On the Confederate side, one recent historian reviewed 1,000 enlistment records and found that about 20 percent were below 19. Of these, one was 13, three were 14, 31 were 15, 200 were 16, and 336 were 17. These studies would suggest, by extrapolation, that about 72,000 "boys" (26,000 Union and 36,000 Confederate) gave service in the war, about 1.9 percent of the total troops that served in the war.

In most states, the legal age for enlisting was 18. Quite often patriotic and zealous young men who were underage managed to enlist when they appeared older or recruiting agents looked the other way. A common dodge was for an underage potential recruit to put a slip of paper in his shoes with the number "18" written on it. Then he could truthfully answer the recruiting officer that he was "over 18."

One of the most famous underage recruits in the war was Arthur MacArthur of Wisconsin. At age 17 he was too young to enlist in 1861, so he took on the non-combat job of regimental adjutant of the 24th Wisconsin. His skills were so great that he was given field command as regimental lieutenant colonel at age 18. In 1863 he won the Congressional Medal of Honor for his heroism at the battle of Missionary Ridge. By 1865 he was a colonel; he eventually rose to the rank of lieutenant general in 1906. Today he is best remembered as the father of General

Children at war: Federal drummer boys.

Douglas MacArthur.

Perhaps the youngest officer in the Union army was Ellis Hamilton of Company F of the 15th New Jersey Infantry. He was born on 15 October, 1845, and enlisted as a 2nd lieutenant in August 1862 at the age of 16 years and 10 months. He rose to the rank of 1st lieutenant just six months later, and was promoted to captain in November 1863 when he was barely 18 years old. Young Hamilton was mortally wounded at the battle of the Wilderness in May 1864. His gravestone in Trenton, New Jersey, appropriately carries the notation, "The Youngest commissioned officer in the Union Army."

Underage recruits were actively sought by both sides, not for the firing line, but for the honorable post of musician. In the noise and din of battle, spoken orders could never be heard, so it was the custom to have orders conveyed by the cadence of drummers or the tunes of fifers. When not utilized as musicians, fifers and drummers also had the distasteful but important task of helping to move the wounded from the battlefield and caring for them in hospitals. Perhaps two-thirds of all Civil War soldiers under the age of 18 were serving legitimately as musicians.

When the war began, there was no lower limit on the age of drummer boys. The youngest Union drummer boy may have been 9-year-old Joseph H. White of the 14th Connecticut. Charles King, drummer boy of the 49th Pennsylvania, was only 12 years old when he was mortally wounded at the battle of Antietam. The youngest Confederate casualty in the war may have been Private George Larkin of the Mississippi Artillery, wounded at the battle of Shiloh when he was 12. The Union Army in 1864 fixed the minimum age for a drummer boy at age 16; the Confederate Army never set any age limit for its musicians.

Drummer boys easily became mascots or "pets" in their regiments. Quite often they enlisted with a family member or close friend, and were permitted to join the troops on the firing line when they reached age 18. Until that time, the young drummer boys thoroughly enjoyed their soldier life with its opportunities for adventure, play, and learning to drink, smoke, and cuss.

The most famous of the young Civil War drummer boys was Johnny Clem. Clem supposedly enlisted at age 10 as drummer of the 22nd Michigan. He won national attention as "Johnny Shiloh" for his heroism at that battle after his drum was shattered by a shell. Later, he reportedly shot and killed a Confederate colonel at Chickamauga, a deed for which he was also called "Drummer Boy of Chickamauga."

Recent research suggests that Clem may have fabricated the stories of his famous war exploits. His enlistment papers still survive, and they show he did not enlist until May 1863, over a year after Shiloh. Close study of the battle of Chickamauga shows that no Confederate colonels were killed in the area where Clem's regiment fought. Regardless of how true Clem's wartime escapades were, the fame he gained from them enabled him to make the army his career. He retired in 1916 at the rank of major general.

The heroic deeds of at least 20 underage soldiers were better attested than those of "Johnny Shiloh." Following are the brief stories of a few of the drummer boys and teenage soldiers who were among the 152 winners of the Congressional Medal of Honor during the Civil War.

Orion P. Howe of the 55th Illinois was 14 years old when he received his medal for heroism at Vicksburg. During an attack on 19 May, his regiment was pinned down and low on ammunition. Howe volunteered to go for more ammo, and was badly wounded on the mission. When he reached his own lines he reported personally to General Sherman. By mistake, Howe requested the wrong size ammunition. But that didn't matter because Sherman forgot to order it up any way.

The youngest Union Medal of Honor winner was 11-year-old Willie Johnston of the 3rd Vermont. He won recognition for being reportedly the only drummer boy to bring his drum unharmed through the 1862 Peninsula Campaign.

John Cooke, 15-year-old bugler in the 4th U.S. Artillery, won a medal for helping to man a cannon at the battle of Antietam. Young Willie Magee of the 33rd New Jersey won his medal for helping to drag off two captured cannons during the battle of Murfreesboro.

The Confederate Army also had its share of brave teenage soldiers. Private John Sloan of the 9th Texas was 13 years old when he lost a leg at the battle of Shiloh. T.D. Clairborne became a captain in the 18th Virginia when he was only 14. He was a lieutenant colonel when he died of wounds in 1864 at the age of 17. An officer from North Carolina once praised 13 year old William Cain of the Hillsboro Military Academy for being one of the best drill masters in the Confederate Army. Two underage Confederate soldiers, 14 year old Robert W. Davis of Florida and 15-year-old John W. Maddox of Georgia, became U.S. congressmen after the war.

Because of chronic manpower shortages, Confederate officials at times had to make use of teenage cadets from Southern military academies. Cadets from The Citadel in Charleston were present at the bombardment of Fort Sumter in 1861, and helped defend their city from Sherman in 1865. The war's most famous use of teenage troops came when the boy cadets of the Virginia Military Institute were called out to defend the Shenandoah Valley in the spring of 1864. Some 258 boy cadets, almost every one under age 18, found themselves actively engaged at the battle of New Market on 15 May, 1864. The cadets charged across a muddy field as bravely as any veteran troops and helped capture an enemy battery, losing 8 killed and 26 wounded in the attack.

The image of heroic young drummer boys became very popular in war time and postwar art and music. Will S. Hays' "The Drummer Boy of Shiloh" became very popular on the home front, and Dr. Francis O. Tickner's poem "Little Giffer" was memorized by a generation of students.

The Union navy got its revenge a month later at the battle of Memphis. Halleck's occupation of Corinth, Mississippi, at the end of May had left Memphis and Fort Pillow open to land attack, so the Confederates withdrew their defending forces on 4 June. They did, however, keep their River Defense Fleet at Memphis in order to prevent the Yankee fleet from advancing downstream toward Vicksburg. The Confederate boats were attacked on 6 June by the bulk of the Union fleet, now under command of Captain Charles H. Davis (Admiral Foote had been badly wounded at Fort Donelson). Davis won the battle, aided greatly by special rams designed and commanded by Colonel Charles Ellet; Ellet himself was mortally wounded in the action. Ellet's son, Lieutenant Charles R. Ellet, received the surrender of Memphis the next day, 7 June.

The fall of Memphis sent a shudder all the way to Vicksburg. That fortress, however, was spared pressure from the north that summer because of other developments farther east. In early June, Halleck decided to break up his large army. His force was big enough to advance on Vicksburg and take it, but he feared other Confederate forces operating in his rear. By Halleck's orders, Pope's Army of the Mississippi kept an eye on Beauregard's army in Mississippi while Buell moved his Army of the Ohio towards Chattanooga. Grant and his Army of the Tennessee of about 60,000 were assigned to guard all the railroads between Corinth, Memphis and Columbus. Any thoughts Grant had of moving South were curtailed in August when he was ordered to send a substantial part of his command to face Confederate General Braxton Bragg's invasion of Kentucky.

Commander of Federal armies in the West during the battles of Fort Henry, Fort Donelson and Shiloh, Henry W. Halleck. In July of 1862, Halleck became General-in-Chief of the Federal Armies.

On the second day of Shiloh, Grant's army assumes the offensive and retakes the earlier gains of the Confederates.

Corinth, Mississippi, during Beauregard's evacuation of the town in May 1862.

CHAPTER II

THE FALL OF NEW ORLEANS

While the people of Vicksburg kept their attention fixed on Grant's Union threat from the north, a new and critical threat suddenly arose from the south. This threat was totally unexpected because of the great faith held in the Mississippi River defenses south of New Orleans. The main line of defense consisted of two star shaped-forts about 30 miles from the ocean and 70 miles south of the Crescent City. These two forts with their 1200 men and 70 guns commanded a bend on the river: Fort Jackson was on the West Bank and Fort St. Philip a little bit to the north on the east bank. Between the two forts was a barrier of sunken small boats linked by iron chains stretched from shore to shore.

The barrier and forts were supported by a small but motley fleet that included a ram (the *Manassas*), a 16 gun warship (the *Louisiana*), and assorted steamboats and smaller craft. In case Yankee boats broke through the defenses, a small fleet of fire boats lay ready for use. Confederate morale was high based on memories of 1815 when the city rallied to drive back British invaders.

It was also unthinkable to the citizens of New Orleans that their cosmopolitan city, the largest city and the banking center of the South, could ever fall into enemy hands. But it was exactly these characteristics that attracted Northern attention. The port of New Orleans had been one of the first objects of the Union saltwater blockade proposed as part of General Winfield Scott's Anaconda Plan. The blockade managed to stop the city's foreign trade since British and French ships were reluctant to pass it, but it by no means stopped all blockade runners in those early days. Nevertheless, the docks of New Orleans became quiet as virtually all trade ceased and cotton bales piled up uselessly in warehouses. Things soon got so bad that everyone simply hoped for the war to go away and things to return to normal. As one citizen put it, "The blockade had closed in like a prison-gate; . . . the city that had once believed it was to be the greatest in the world, was absolutely out of employment."

The plan for the conquest of New Orleans was drawn up in November 1861 by Admiral David Dixon Porter. His strategy was straight forward. He would equip a flotilla of mortar boats (small sailing vessels that each carried a 13-inch mortar) and use them to reduce Forts Jackson and St. Philip into submission. Then a squadron of warships commanded by David G. Farragut would be able to sail up to force the surrender of New Orleans. Accompanying Farragut would be an army force of at least 20,000 men for use as garrisons throughout Louisiana.

If all went well, Porter urged, a quick dash could also be made up river to Vicksburg or Memphis, to link up with Admiral Foote's fleet coming downstream. Thus the capture of New Orleans would also lead to the speedy conquest of the entire Mississippi Valley.

After two months of preparations, the expedition left New York and Philadelphia in late January. The 19 mortar boats rendezvoused a month later at the jumping off base at Ship Island, located in the Gulf of Mexico off the coast of Mississippi about 60 miles east of New Orleans. Once most of the 24 warships arrived that were assigned to the expedition, the fleet embarked for its first obstacle, crossing the natural sandbars at the mouth of the Mississippi. It was easy enough for steamboats to tow the mortar boats over the sandbars on March 18. The deep water warships had much greater difficulty passing over these obstacles. With naval persistence and ingenuity, the whole fleet was finally brought into the Mississippi after almost two weeks of labor. It was indeed a bold move to bring such a large-ocean going fleet into the river, but the move was necessary in order to accomplish the purpose of the expedition. Only later did Porter lament that he had not insisted on bringing along an ironclad warship or two. They would have been of great assistance in the heavy fighting to come.

Porter now began proceeding cautiously upstream toward Forts Jackson and St. Philip, some 30-odd miles upstream. He reached his goal on 16 April. After taking a day to scout the Confederate positions, Porter turned his mortar boats loose on the morning of 18 April. The barrage took the Confederates totally unaware as the mortars lobbed 240 shells an hour on the forts. They simply had not realized that Porter had brought along so many mortars of such large size. The Confederates tried to return the Yankee fire, but could not see their targets to get the range; Porter had kept his mortar boats out of sight on a river bend and had camouflaged their mast tops with tree branches.

One of America's greatest naval commanders, David Glasgow Farragut (l.) aboard the Hartford. Farragut, also known as "Daring Dave," was responsible for spectacular victories at New Orleans and Mobile Bay.

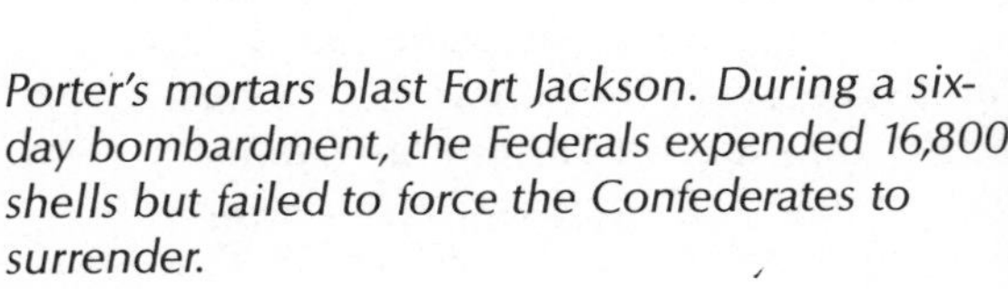

Porter's mortars blast Fort Jackson. During a six-day bombardment, the Federals expended 16,800 shells but failed to force the Confederates to surrender.

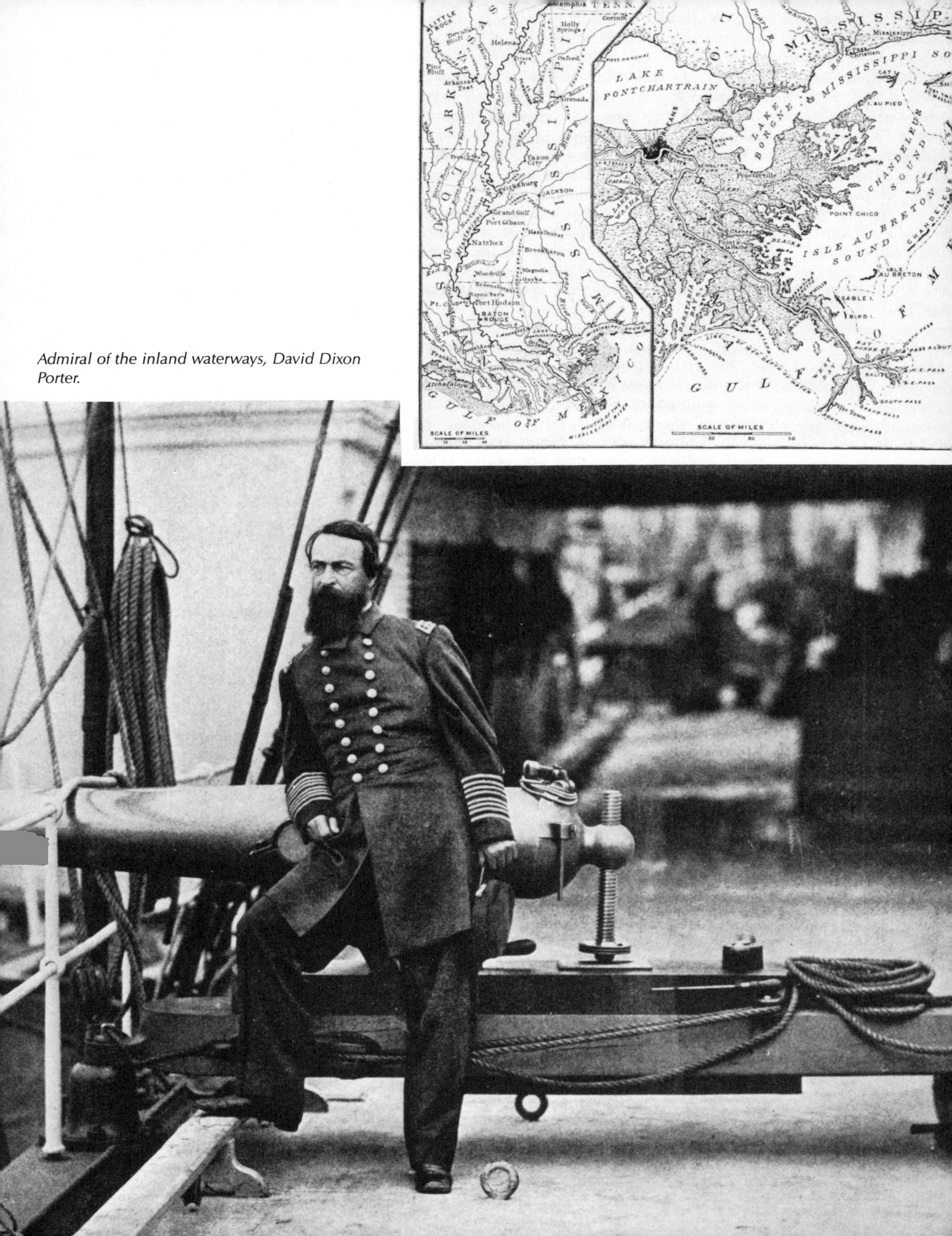

Admiral of the inland waterways, David Dixon Porter.

When the Confederates showed no sign of surrender, Porter maintained his bombardment for six straight days. It was one of the greatest artillery bombardments of the war, with over 16,800 shells fired. One Union observer wrote of the din, "Combine all that you have heard of thunder, add to it all you have ever seen of lightning, and you have, perhaps, a conception of the scene."

The Confederate forts were badly battered by the bombardment, and a fire that broke out in Fort Jackson for a time encouraged the bombarders. Exhausted as they were, the Confederate defenders refused to consider surrender while their defenses were still intact. They were greatly relieved on 22 April when Porter finally had to call off the bombardment due to declining ammunition supply. Porter was embarrassed that his mission had not been accomplished, putting the whole expedition in jeopardy. General Ben Butler, commander of Porter's land forces, was at a loss about what to do next. Admiral Farragut, commander of the warships, was particularly annoyed since Porter had assured him the Confederates would surrender after two days of bombardment.

Farragut was not one to sit still during such a crisis (he was the one who would exclaim "Damn the torpedoes, full speed ahead!" at the battle of Mobile Bay in August 1864). Here at New Orleans, Farragut made the brash decision to run his warships right past the Confederate forts, hitting strength with strength. The proposal was doubly dangerous because any lost warships would weaken the saltwater blockading squadron, which had been stripped in order to provide vessels for the New Orleans expedition. Porter argued that it would be a disaster to try to run by the forts, especially since that would entail abandoning his mortar boats below the forts. By no one cared for the noisy but ineffective mortar boats, so Porter's warnings were not heeded.

Before proceeding past the forts, Farragut had to deal first with the boom of boats that blockaded the river channel. Two brave boats, the *Itasca* and the *Pinola*, volunteered to undertake what was viewed as a suicide mission. They waited for darkness on the 22nd, and sailed up to the boom under heavy enemy fire. Volunteers used great hammers and chisels on the iron chain that held the boom together. At length a link was broken and with it the chain, flinging its two arms and the Yankee boats towards the shore, and opening the river for Farragut's warships.

Farragut directed his attack to begin at 0200 on 24 April. His first orders were for his 17 warships to proceed in single file behind the flagship, *Hartford*. His commanders talked him out of this foolishness, persuading him that it was senseless for the commander to draw the first fury of the enemy fire. Farragut's revised orders put the *Cayuga* first in line, with the *Hartford* in the middle of the procession. All

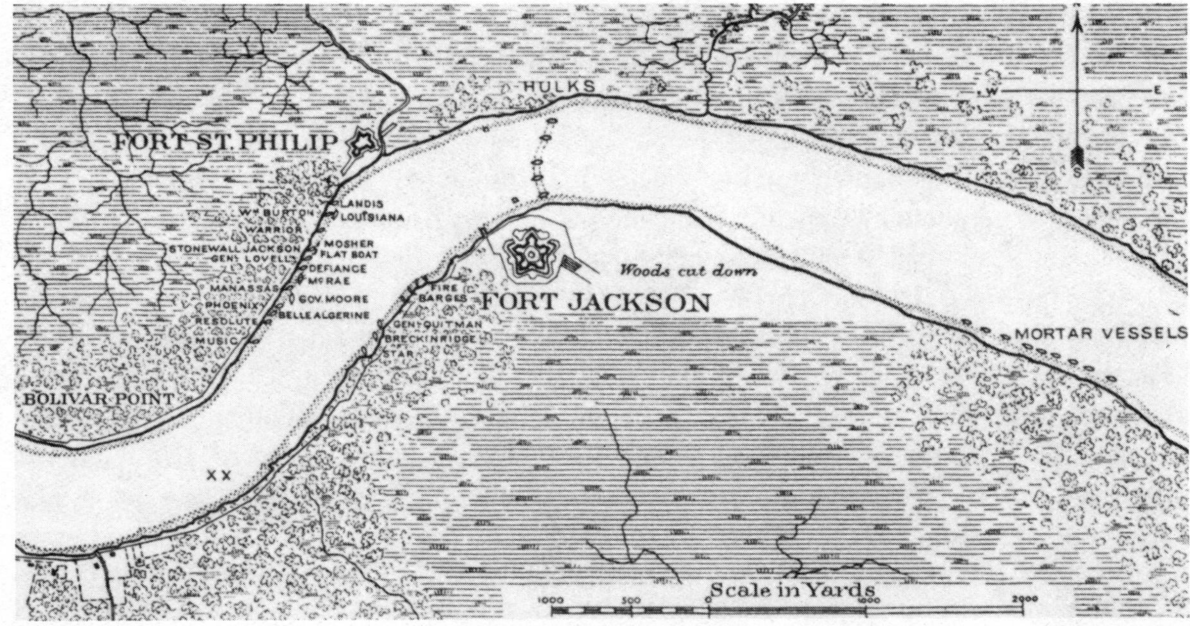

Map showing the defenses below New Orleans as well as the position of Porter's mortar-boats.

boats were to protect their engine rooms by dropping chains over their sides. Farragut expected to take heavy casualties in the attack, perhaps as high as fifty percent.

The movement began as scheduled at 0200. Because of the strong current, it took the leading ship, the *Cayuga*, until 0245 to draw near to the Confederate forts. The Confederates had expected something was happening when some of their boats heard Union anchors being winched up, so the Southerners were ready at their guns. The instant the *Cayuga* was visible through the darkness, all hell broke loose. Both Confederate forts plus all their boats opened fire. Farragut's boats responded, supported by Porter's mortar boats. Porter himself later wrote of the scene, "From almost perfect silence, one incessant roar of heavy cannon commenced. . . . the bombshells crossed each other and exploded in the air, it seemed as if a battle was taking place in the heavens as well as on earth."

Farragut's warships blasted away at the Confederate forts as they passed, receiving heavy but not incapacitating damage. The greatest danger to the Union fleet was posed by the Confederate river rams, which were well equipped for their work. One of these, the *Moore*, rammed the warship *Varuna* and sent her to the bottom before being cornered and sunk herself. The biggest Confederate ram was the Manassas. It crashed into the Union warship *Brooklyn*, and left a gaping hole before it backed off. Fortunately for the *Brooklyn*, the hole in her hull was temporarily blocked when the coal cargo shifted towards the point of impact. The *Manassas* was not so lucky as she got stuck on a mudbank while trying to escape the USS *Mississippi*. Farragut's men were also fortunate that the commander of the Confederate ironclad *Louisiana* chose not to enter the fight actively. The commander did not trust the power of his engines, so he kept his warship tied to the bank as a floating battery. Had he been able to enter action, the *Louisiana* would have caused as much damage as the *Merrimac* (*Virginia*) did at Hampton Roads in March 1862 before stopped by the *Monitor*.

The most critical moment of the battle arrived when the Confederates upstream released fire rafts, which immediately bore down on the Union fleet. One of these struck Farragut's flagship, the *Hartford*, and was pinned there by a brave Confederate tugboat. For a moment it looked like the *Hartford* would go up in flames. Farragut kept his composure and directed bucket brigades to put out the fires. Meanwhile he blasted the pesky tugboat until it sank.

The Confederate ram Manassas smashes into the USS Brooklyn. Despite the blow, the Brooklyn managed to stay afloat.

Admirals of the Inland Seas

Victor of Fort Henry, Andrew Foote.

David Porter (l.) with General George Meade of Gettysburg fame.

Probably the best U.S. Naval commander during the Civil War, "Daring Dave" Farragut.

A significant contributing factor to the Union success in the Vicksburg campaign was the skill and enterprise of the North's naval commanders. This is not to deny that the North had superior boats and armament throughout the campaign. It is important to note that these boats would not have been used as successfully as they were had their naval leaders been as unskilled as some of their counterparts on land. In addition, the Union cause was aided by the high degree of cooperation between Grant and the top naval officers.

The success of Grant's initial drive through Tennessee in the spring of 1862 was aided greatly by the support of Admiral Andrew Hull Foote, commander of Union naval forces on the upper Mississippi. Foote was born in New Haven, Connecticut, in 1806. He at first attended West Point, but then transferred to Annapolis, which was more to his liking. During his lengthy pre-Civil War service, he was noted for his aggressiveness as much as for his strong feelings against alcohol and slavery. Foote was appointed to his Midwestern command in August 1861. He got along very well with Grant, though he stole some of Grant's thunder by capturing Fort Henry on 6 February 1862, before Grant's land forces could arrive. During the successful attack on Fort Donelson, Foote was badly wounded in the foot by a shell. He continued in command through Pope's capture of Island No. 10. He then had to retire from field service because of his wound. Foote held a desk job in Washington, D.C., for a year, but yearned to return to the sea. In mid-1863 he was given command of the South Atlantic Blockading Squadron. However, he died while en route to his post, at the age of 57.

David Dixon Porter, commander of the Mississippi Squadron at New Orleans and Vicksburg, was born in Chester, Pennsylvania, in 1813, to a distinguished family—his father was a career naval officer, his brother William became an admiral, his cousin Fitz John Porter was a noted general early in the war, and his adopted brother was none other than David G. Farragut, his assistant commander during the New Orleans campaign. Porter first went to sea at age ten, and literally worked his way through the ranks, despite his family connections. His first Civil War service came as commander of the ship *Powhatan* stationed at Pensacola. It was Porter who developed the plans for the capture of New Orleans and then lobbied in Washington for their acceptance. He was rewarded for his efforts with command of the naval forces attacking New Orleans. Though his initial plan of bombarding Forts Jackson and St. Philip into surrender failed, he did finally gain the submission when Farragut occupied New Orleans.

In October Porter was given command of the Mississippi River squadron operating north of Vicksburg (Foote's old command). He cooperated so well with the Union land forces

After sinking the Varuna, the Governor Moore receives a destructive broadside from the Pensacola.

during the capture of Arkansas Post in January 1863 and Vicksburg in July that he was promoted to rear admiral. His skills and patience were tested to the extreme when he led his fleet to accompany Banks' dismal Red River campaign in the spring of 1864. Afterwards he requested a transfer away from the inland waters back to the ocean. He received command of the North Atlantic Blockading Squadron. In the attack on Fort Fisher at the very end of 1864, Porter commanded a fleet of 44 warships, the largest ever assembled under the U.S. flag to that time.

After the war, Porter's reputation was so great that he was appointed superintendent of the Naval Academy. He was promoted to Full Admiral in 1870. Admiral Porter died in Washington D.C. in 1891 at the age of 77.

David Glasglow Farragut, one of the war's most colorful naval commanders, was born in Tennessee in 1801. He was adopted at an early age by the influential Porter family that included his fellow admiral-to-be, David Dixon Porter. Farragut had a full and lengthy pre-Civil War service record, as he fought in the War of 1812 as a midshipman before he reached his teens.

Farragut was a resident of Virginia and had a wife from Norfolk when the Civil War began. His allegiance was nevertheless with the Union, and in December 1861 Navy Secretary Gideon Welles trusted him enough to give him command of the West Gulf Blockading Squadron. In this command he was assigned to assist his adoptive brother David D. Porter in the capture of Ship Island, the base for the campaign, in December. He then boldly ran his fleet past Forts Jackson and St. Philip on 24 April, and pushed on to accept the surrender of New Orleans. For this act he was promoted to rear admiral and was voted the thanks of Congress.

Farragut participated in the early unsuccessful attempts to capture Vicksburg in late 1862 and the beginning of 1863. He then turned his attention back to his blockading squadron. Here his main goal was the capture of Mobile, Alabama, one of the few uncaptured Confederate ports. He attacked Mobile with all his force on 5 August 1864. Mobile's harbor was mined with torpedoes, which caused Farragut's men great discomfort. In a show of courage, Farragut lashed himself to the rigging of his longtime flagship, the *Hartford*, and uttered his now memorable order, "Damn the torpedoes! Full speed ahead!" His brave action helped win the battle, and brought about the surrender of Mobile later in the month; for his deeds he was promoted to rear admiral.

After the war, Farragut was promoted to full admiral in command of the European Squadron. He passed away in Portsmouth, New Hampshire, in 1870 at the age of 69.

J.O. DAVIDSON

Farragut's fleet defies deadly cannon fire from Fort Jackson, Fort St. Philip and Confederate vessels and plows on to its objective, the Crescent City, New Orleans.

Benjamin Butler.

The man who lost New Orleans, Mansfield Lovell.

In possession of New Orleans, Yankees remove the state flag from city hall.

CHAPTER III

THE THREATS BECOME REAL

On 1 May 1862, Union Major General Ben "Beast" Butler and his 15,000 infantry finally reached New Orleans and took the city from Farragut's sailors and marines. Farragut was anxious to push on and take Baton Rouge, Natchez and Vicksburg, but would have to do so without substantial infantry support. Butler wanted to occupy New Orleans in force, and loaned the navy only 1,400 men under Brigadier General Thomas Williams to be used in operations farther north.

Farragut divided his warships into two flotillas for his dash upstream. The advance flotilla, commanded by Captain S. Phillips Lee of the *Oneida*, was to hurry forward to grab Vicksburg. The trailing squadron, led by Commander James S. Palmer aboard the *Iroquois*, easily took possession of Baton Rouge and Natchez. Meanwhile, Captain Phillips was pushing on to Vicksburg, which he reached 18 May.

Phillips expected Vicksburg to be lightly defended, a plum ripe for the plucking, and indeed it would have been so had he reached the town a month earlier. Instead, much to his surprise, he found the town defended by a strong force of 18 guns manned by veteran artillerists and supported by almost 4,000 infantry. The presence of this garrison was the strategy of Major General Mansfield Lovell, Confederate commander who had recently lost New Orleans. Lovell had decided that the Crescent City was indefensible after Farragut ran his fleet past Forts Jackson and St. Philip. Instead of wasting his men in battle against Butler's much larger Union force, Lovell evacuated New Orleans as soon as Farragut arrived there, and shipped his valuable men north by railroad to Jackson. From Jackson, the troops were sent west to Vicksburg.

Farragut was badly shaken by this incident and by the pounding his boats were taking. He had put his career on the line by his bold decision, but for the moment he feared most for his ships and his men. As dawn lightened the skies, he was relieved to see that things had turned out better than he expected. Only one boat, the *Varuna*, had been sunk, though two others were badly damaged and three had turned back from the forts. Altogether about 200 sailors were casualties. Confederate losses were not as heavy, but they had lost their entire flotilla except for two boats. Most importantly, Farragut now had 13 intact warships north of the forts, with a clear path to New Orleans.

Farragut's reduced fleet steamed on toward New Orleans, leaving Porter and his gunboats to deal with Forts Jackson and St. Philip. The only opposition Farragut faced on his voyage was a few shots from a couple Confederate batteries at Chalmette, the source of Andrew Jackson's 1815 victory just below the Crescent City. As soon as the New Orleans merchants heard of Farragut's approach, many set fire to their warehouses and the cotton stored on the wharves. These fires burned all night despite a heavy rain.

Farragut reached New Orleans aboard the *Hartford* on 25 April to find the streets subdued and under a smokey pall from the dock fires. There was no military opposition because Confederate Major General Mansfield Lovell had evacuated the town. When Farragut sent a delegation to the town's mayor to demand surrender, it returned empty handed. This put the Admiral in an awkward situation. Despite the town's defenselessness, he did not have any troops with him to take possession of it, since he had left all of Butler's troops with Porter back at Forts Jackson and St. Philip.

The situation created a curious impasse. Farragut's fleet at New Orleans was unable to occupy the city without troops, and the troops were

Martin L. Smith.

held at Forts Jackson and St. Philip, which refused to surrender despite continued bombardment from Porter's mortar boats. The impasse held until 28 April, when the Confederate commanders at the two forts finally decided to call it quits. Their forts were still intact and supplied with ammunition, but their troops were getting weary and dispirited because of Farragut's presence at New Orleans. Negotiations came close to a halt when Porter's flagship the *Harriet Lane* was almost blown up by the Confederate ironclad *Louisiana*, that drifted by after being set afire by her crew. It took quite awhile for an irate Porter to accept that the *Louisiana* had not been sent to attack him, but was poorly scuttled by her crew. The delayed surrender of Forts Jackson and St. Philip gave Farragut the impetus to move some men into New Orleans. Since he knew heavy reinforcements would soon reach him that same day, 28 April, he landed a battalion of marines and took possession of the New Orleans custom house and city hall.

The arrival of Lovell's troops turned Vicksburg into an armed camp, and stiffened the resolve of its citizens, who were still in shock over the sudden loss of New Orleans. On 12 May, Lovell assigned Brigadier General Martin L. Smith to personally oversee the preparation of the city's defenses. Smith established seven batteries on the high bluffs above the river, all manned by veterans of the fight at New Orleans. To reinforce his command, Smith called out the members of the Vicksburg area militia on 15 May. These citizen soldiers between the ages of 18 and 50 formed at the courthouse and were put under the command of Charles E. Smedes, a local grocer with the exalted rank of brigadier general of militia.

Thus the town of Vicksburg was ready and well defended when Captain Phillips and his seven boats steamed into view from the south on Sunday 18 May 1862. Phillips anchored his flagship *Oneida*, and dispatched a small boat to demand the surrender of the city. When a shot from the bluffs flew past her bow the small boat hesitated. She was met by a Confederate steamboat, which carried Phillips' demand to General Smith: "The undersigned, with orders from Flag Officer Farragut and Major General Butler, respectively, demand the surrender of Vicksburg and its defenses to the lawful authority of the United States, under which private property and personal rights will be respected."

By nightfall, Phillips had not one but three refusals to surrender the city. Laz Lindsay, mayor of Vicksburg, asserted that "neither the municipal authorities nor the citizens will ever consent to a surrender of the city." Lindsay was supported by Colonel James L. Autry, who sent Phillips a challenge: "Mississippians don't know, and refuse to learn, how to surrender. If Commodore Farragut or Brigadier General Butler can teach them, let them come and try." General Smith, who commanded most of the troops in town and so would have had the greatest say on the question of surrender, responded simply and to the point, "Having been ordered to hold these defenses, it is my intention to do so."

The strength of Vicksburg's defenses and the determination of her defenders made Phillips realize the precariousness of his situation—the force he had with him was not large enough to capture the city, which appeared to be receiving reinforcements daily. Phillips for all practical purposes knew he had to wait until the rest of Farragut's fleet reached him. Then it might be possible to reduce the city by cannonade. Meanwhile, Phillips decided to try a bold ruse. He sent a message to Mayor Lindsay on the 21st to surrender or he would bombard the town in 24 hours; in view of this threat, the naval commander advised that Vicksburg's women and children be evacuated to places of safety.

Phillips' threat did not elicit much response from Mayor Lindsay, who, of course, still refused to surrender. Most of the private citizens who remained in town simply headed for the shelter of their basements; the citizens who were weak at heart had left town when the first news arrived of the fall of New Orleans. Everyone expected Phillips' boats to open fire on the evening of 22 May, but the appointed hour came and went. Three additional days passed, but nothing happened, even though Phillips was heavily reinforced by the rest of Farragut's fleet.

At length the Union naval commanders decided that they had to make at least one attempt to bombard Vicksburg into submission. They knew they did not have enough land troops to assault the city—in fact, General Williams' 1400 men aboard the transports were probably just barely adequate to garrison the city if it could be induced to surrender. There was always the chance that a show of aggressive force might

Men who "didn't know how to surrender" and "refused to learn," Southern soldiers from Mississippi.

discourage the Confederate defenders, or might disable enough of their cannons to persuade them to surrender.

The time chosen for the naval bombardment was 1700 on Monday, 26 May. The ships moved into position and began firing, but retired after firing only about twenty rounds. (The purpose of the maneuver may have been to get the proper range for the naval guns). The next day the fleet again sailed up, and began firing at 1500. This time the Yankees were in earnest, and maintained their fire for twelve hours.

The 27 May bombardment was a serious one, but not as heavy as what the city would see a year later during Grant's siege. This one was nevertheless well remembered by the inhabitants of Vicksburg because it was the first of the kind they ever saw. One young lad later wrote how this bombardment especially affected him as he crouched near the coal pile in his basement with his mother, sisters, and negro slave praying for safety: "The war became to me for the first time a reality, and not the fairy tale it had hitherto seemed."

The houses of Vicksburg received a fair amount of damage during this cannonade, but the town was in no mood to surrender. In fact, few Confederate guns had even bothered to reply to the Union bombardment. Most held their fire for the expected infantry attack. When this never came and the bombardment finally ceased, the defenders breathed a great sigh of relief. A few families, especially those with children, took the opportunity to move to safer locations at plantations outside the city.

Farragut now had to admit that he was stymied. He did not have enough guns to overwhelm the city; in fact, the 200-foot river bluffs were so high that many of his guns could not get sufficient elevation to even hit the Confederate defenses. The admiral vented most of his wrath on Butler for refusing to loan him enough infantry to attack the fortress. He then made the difficult decision of calling off the expedition, which had begun so gloriously below New Orleans. Farragut had a great fear that the waters of the Mississippi might recede during summertime heat and strand his oceangoing warships in mud. Reluctantly, he left six gunboats below Vicksburg and turned south with his five biggest warships.

Farragut was not one to take defeat easily. As soon as he arrived in New Orleans, he set about organizing a second, stronger expedition against Vicksburg. He planned to take along over 3,000 infantry, plus some light field batteries. Most importantly, he would also bring along Porter's mortar boats, which would have the trajectory and range to reach Vicksburg's battlements on the bluffs.

Farragut's armada left New Orleans at the very end of May, and proceeded north with only a few minor incidents. His flagship, the *Hartford*, ran aground briefly below Natchez, and Confederate guerrillas along the river banks took shots at the fleet whenever they could. Farragut also had to be wary of the Confederate guns on the bluffs at Grand Gulf, some 60 miles below Vicksburg. The admiral dealt with this threat by landing a few infantry regiments which burned down most of the small town.

Farragut's flagship, the Hartford.

Farragut reached Vicksburg on 25 June and began preparation for a bombardment. He then received news that changed his whole approach to the situation. Commander Charles H. Davis, commander of Foote's former squadron on the upper Mississippi, had finally captured Fort Pillow and Memphis, and was now only 20 miles north of Vicksburg. Since Farragut had orders to link up with Davis if he could, he decided to run his fleet north past Vicksburg, just as he had done at Forts Jackson and St. Philip. In preparation for the movement, he established communications with Davis' fleet by sending messengers by land across the Desoto Peninsula in Arkansas, which was west of the Mississippi and so not in the control of Vicksburg's defenders.

Farragut's fleet at a coaling station in Baton Rouge during his naval assault on the city in mid-1862.

Farragut ordered his movement for 0200 on 28 June. In preparation for it, he ordered his mortar boats to open fire on the afternoon of 26 June. They kept up their fire for the next two days, supported by field artillery placed on DeSoto Point. Just as at Forts Jackson and St. Philip, the mortars caused more noise than damage. Confederate Colonel S.H. Lokett, chief engineer at Vicksburg, described the effects of this bombardment as follows: "At a signal gun from one of the iron clads the guns were opened. I measured one of the holes made by the mortar shells in hard, compact clay, and found it seventeen feet deep. It was a difficult matter to make bomb proofs against such destructive engines. A few shots were fired from our batteries in answer to the challenge of the mortar boats but these shots were harmless, and were soon discontinued. The Federal bombardment was likewise nearly harmless. But few soldiers and citizens were killed. Vertical fire is never very destructive of life. Yet the howling and bursting shells had a very demoralizing effect on those not accustomed to them. One of my engineer officers, a Frenchman, a gallant officer who had distinguished himself in several severe engagements, was almost unmanned whenever one passed anywhere near him. When joked about it, he was not ashamed to confess: 'I no like ze bomb; I cannot fight him back!'"

At the appointed hour of 0200 on 28 June, Farragut raised two red lanterns on the mast of his flagship, the *Hartford*, as a signal for this fleet to proceed. The ships were spotted by Vicksburg's batteries at 0400, and another horrendous bombardment commenced. Vicksburg's 29 heavy guns fired as fast as they could, answered by all the guns of Farragut's fleet, supported by the mortar boats and the land batteries on DeSoto Point. The noise of the bombardment caused a tremendous scare in the

One of the mortars bombarding Vicksburg unleashes its deadly load during 26 June bombardment. Despite making a deafening racket, these guns did little to hasten the surrender of the Confederate town.

Federal vessel on patrol on the Mississippi.

town, where many citizens took flight and headed west to escape the Yankee bombs. One poor woman, Mrs. Alice Gramble, never made it to safety. She was struck and killed by a shell, the first citizen of Vicksburg to be killed in what would become a long Roll of Honor.

The *Richmond* was the first ship to meet the fire of Vicksburg's guns. By 0430 she was in the worst of it, but she made it through after suffering only a few hits. The ships behind her had similar experiences—some were hit badly, but none were sunk. One of the most badly hit was the *Hartford*. Its captain's cabin was blown apart, and Admiral Farragut's favorite perch was smashed by a shell just seconds after he moved to another part of the ship. The coming of daylight helped the Confederates see their targets better, but this was not enough. By then most of the Yankee fleet had successfully run the gauntlet of the batteries. When Farragut counted his losses, he found only 16 killed and 45 wounded. All his ships but three had made it through; the *Brooklyn* and two other boats had been turned back and now remained south of Vicksburg with the mortar boats and infantry transports. Confederate losses during the engagement were only two killed and three wounded.

Running the Vicksburg batteries was a brave and glorious deed, but it actually did not accomplish a great deal. Farragut's juncture with Davis' four ironclads and six mortar boats carried out his orders from Washington but actually brought Vicksburg's demise no closer. If anything, Farragut's act put the Yankees in a more awkward situation, since Porter's mortar boats were now stranded south of Vicksburg. What was really needed was 10,000 to 15,000 more infantry to take the fortress, for naval guns clearly could not do the task by themselves. Farragut telegraphed bluntly to Washington: "The forts have been passed, and we have done it, and can do it again as often as may be required of us. It will not, however, be an easy matter for us to do more than silence the batteries for a time, as long as the enemy has a large force behind the hills to prevent our landing and holding the place."

While they waited for reinforcements, Farragut decided to keep busy by digging a canal across the base of the DeSoto peninsula. If the canal worked, his boats could sail back and forth freely and ignore Vicksburg's batteries. Building the canal, however, would be a long process (see sidebar). Meanwhile, his troops began to suffer under the sultry Southern sun, and hospital lists grew daily from malaria and other maladies.

Farragut celebrated the 4th of July by ordering a 21-gun salute from his boats. He then approached Vicksburg in the ironclad *Benton* to see how she performed under fire. The Confederates that day were testing a new rifled Whitworth cannon, and were having good luck at hitting the *Benton*. Farragut could not stand the heat of the boat, and exclaimed to Commander Davis, "Dammit, I must go on deck! I

feel as though I were shut up here in an iron pot, and I can't stand it." The admiral found the open deck a bit unsafe, so he finally sought the comparative safety of the ship's pilot house.

Farragut's 4 July foray was the most exciting event at Vicksburg for a couple weeks. The Confederates, though heavily reinforced to 15,000, were growing weary of the daily bombardment from the mortar boats. This lessened after 10 July, when Porter left under orders to take twelve of the mortar boats to Virginia. This did not bother Farragut a great deal, since the mortar boats had not proven themselves to be particularly effective during the campaign. What bothered him more was the fact that the river level was dropping and might soon strand his big warships like the *Hartford* and *Brooklyn* high and dry.

Another of Farragut's formidable vessels, the Brooklyn.

The First Vicksburg Canal

Union naval officers were aware before the 1862 drive on Vicksburg began that the Confederate fortress stood on bluffs at a great bend of the Mississippi River. This bend formed a large peninsula called DeSoto Point that was directly opposite Vicksburg. A canal across the base of DeSoto Point had the potential of diverting the Mississippi away from Vicksburg, making it possible for river traffic to travel out of danger of Vicksburg's batteries.

The plan adopted called for a canal one-and-one-half miles long to be dug across DeSoto Point from a spot six miles upstream of Vicksburg to an outlet three-and-one-half miles below the town. It was to be made 50 feet wide and deep enough for the boats to pass. The whole project was to be supervised by Brigadier General Williams, who would use his own troops as laborers. Supporting them would be about 2000 Blacks "borrowed" from local plantations and pressed into service.

The project was more easily designed than constructed. The canal's architects figured that it would not be necessary to dig the entire 50-foot breadth of the canal. Instead, a small channel would be cut beginning at the canal's southern end. When this finally tapped into the Mississippi at the northern end of the canal, the river's waters would hopefully flush out the canal's banks as they rushed into it.

This plan sounded good on paper, but failed to account for the river's customary summer drop in level. One of the officers involved, Lieutenant Colonel Richard B. Irwin, described the scene when the canal was finally cut through to the river on July 11: "The cut, originally intended to be 4 feet deep and 5 feet wide, had been excavated through the clay (with much felling of trees and grubbing of roots) to a depth of 13 feet, and a width of 18 feet. . . . The grade was now about 18 inches below the river level, and in a few hours the water was to have been let in. Suddenly the banks began to cave, and before anything could be done to remedy this, the river, falling rapidly, was once more below the bottom of the cut."

General Williams was set back by this disaster, but resolved to dig his canal even deeper, forty feet down if necessary. He calculated the work might take another three months. This job was made even more difficult by the number of men on his sick rolls, since his effective force was down to less than 1000 of his original 3200. Mercifully, the canal project was called off, still incomplete on 26 July, when Farragut's fleet was called to other duty. Constructing the canal had been a good idea, but was not realistically possible because of the difficulty of local geology and the state of that day's technology.

CHAPTER IV

THE SAGA OF THE *ARKANSAS*

The military situation at Vicksburg changed drastically with the sudden appearance of the Confederate ironclad *Arkansas* on the scene in mid-July 1862. The Confederates had a fascination with ironclads as floating invulnerable batteries and rams ever since the *Merrimac* (a.k.a. *Virginia*) had singlehandedly almost destroyed the entire Union wooden blockading fleet at Hampton Roads, Virginia, on 8 March 1862. Since they had only a few ships and limited resources, use of large ironclads provided a ready way to make up for their lack of resources and even possibly tip the scales in their favor. When well built and ably captained, ironclads could be very destructive, as Captain Franklin Buchanan had shown with his *Merrimac*. On the other hand, the ironclads were often heavy, cumbersome, and too underpowered to be effective, as was the case with the *Tennessee* in the defense of New Orleans. Time would soon tell what would be the case with the *Arkansas* in the Mississippi at Vicksburg.

Inner workings of a gunboat.

The *Arkansas* was a twin screw ironclad ram whose construction had been started near Memphis in October 1861. She was scheduled to be completed by the end of the year, but work on her proved so slow that she still was not finished when New Orleans was captured in the spring of 1862. Since Memphis at the same time was under pressure from Foote's Union fleet, it was decided to move the unfinished *Arkansas* south to Greenwood, Mississippi, on the Yazoo River. At the same time a less finished sister of the *Arkansas* had to be left behind and burned in her dry docks. The move proved to be an ill-timed one. Memphis was not to be threatened for over a month. In the meantime the *Arkansas* could have been completed and then used in the defense of Memphis.

When the *Arkansas* was moved, she had her woodwork and deck armor done, but her casemate armor was not finished, nor were her engines and guns installed. Despite the urgency of having her completed to face the Yankee fleets on the Mississippi, she lay untouched at a flooded dockyard for over a month. Finally at the end of May, Captain Isaac N. Brown was ordered to rush to the boat and finish her construction as soon as possible. As Brown readied the *Arkansas*, he was far from impressed with her condition: "It being the season of overflow, I found my new command four miles from dry land. Her condition was not encouraging. The

Captain L.N. Brown, skipper of the Arkansas.

vessel was a mere hull, without armor; the engines were apart; guns without carriages were lying about the deck; a portion of the railroad iron intended as armor was at the bottom of the river, and the other and far greater part was to be sought for in the interior of the country."

Fortunately for the Confederacy, Brown was a man of action who was not easily discouraged. He commandeered a steamboat, the *Capitol*, and fished up the submerged railroad iron with her darricles. He then had the unfinished *Arkansas* towed 110 miles to Yazoo City, an important repair yard that had the needed mechanics, machinery and supplies handy. He converted the *Capitol* into a floating dock and hotel for his workers, and lashed her to the *Arkansas*. A workforce of 200 men was drafted from a nearby army detachment. Work proceeded night and day in 100 degree heat; when workers dropped or grew sick from the heat, they were replaced by others, and the work raced on.

The completion of the *Arkansas* was one of the heroic sagas of the war. Iron rails for the boat's armament were scavenged from all over the state, and had to be dragged 25 miles to the building site from the closest railroad terminal. A great amount of specialized machinery was needed to work on the iron rails, and what was not readily available had to be improvised. Altogether 14 blacksmiths' forges were appropriated from nearby plantations. Drilling machines had to be improvised to pierce the rails for the bolts that would hold them to the boat frame. When a special forge could not be found to bend the rails to fit the curve of the bow and stern, Brown instead nailed boiler plate there. Perhaps the hardest part of the project was constructing the carriages for the boat's ten cannons. These had to be custom designed, and there were no gun carriage manufacturers in the state. After a great deal of hunting, Brown found a business in Jackson to take on and successfully finish the task.

Many elements of the boat's design had to be worked out as construction proceeded. Because of a shortage in casement armament, the iron rails were laid at a 35 degree slant on timber walls that were thicker than originally planned. The pilot house, which stood atop the casemate immediately in front of the funnel, was imperfectly covered with a double thickness of one-inch bar iron.

Despite these challenges and the presence of part of the Yankee fleet only fifty miles away, Brown had the *Arkansas* finished in only five weeks. In mid-June he came face to face with a new problem that had to be dealt with immediately. The Yazoo's water level was dropping so fast that the *Arkansas* would soon be trapped at her docks if she were not moved quickly to deeper water. Brown responded quickly by moving the *Arkansas* downstream on 20 June, even though she was still not one hundred percent finished. This maiden voyage revealed a new unexpected design problem. The boat's two screw propellers had an inclination to stop at odd times. Whenever one stopped, the other would drive the ship in a circle until the idling propeller could be started up again.

It now took Captain Brown three weeks to gather his crew of 232 men. About 100 of these were veterans of the late River Defense Fleet. Another large detachment were plucky Missourians who knew nothing about boating. The ship carried ten cannons placed as follows: two 8-inch 64-pounders at the bow; two rifled 32-pounders at the stern; and two 100-pound Columbiads and a 6-inch naval gun on each broadside. Six of the guns came from Memphis, and four were appropriated from two old gunboats. Altogether the warship and its armament cost $76,920 to construct.

Brown's plan for the *Arkansas* was to proceed to Vicksburg and then make a dash on Memphis in an effort to liberate the city. General Earl Van Dorn had alerted him that the Yankees had 38 warships near Vicksburg, and Brown was prepared to fight his way through them if he had to. He planned on having the element of surprise on his side, and hoped that in the process he might be able to cause significant damage to the Union fleet.

On 12 July Brown set out on a "shakedown cruise" to Satartia, on the Yazoo River 50 miles north of Vicksburg. After reaching Satartia, he readied his boat for action and departed for Vicksburg early on Monday, 14 July. He had proceeded only 15 miles when a leaky boiler sprayed hot water all over his gunpowder supply. Captain Brown had no choice but to put ashore and spread his gunpowder out to dry while anxiously keeping a look out for enemy boats. Another tense moment came late in the day when low hanging trees almost knocked over the boat's smokestack.

Brown rested his men for a few hours after midnight and headed into a branch of the Mississippi shortly before dawn on the 25th. When the sun rose, he spotted a Union patrol heading his way. It consisted of three boats, the iron clad *Carondelet*, the wooden gunboat *Tyler*, and the ram *Queen of the West*. Brown boldly headed for the strongest enemy ship, the *Carondelet*, while he blazed at the other two with his broadside guns. Despite the odds against her, the *Arkansas* began to get the upper hand. Her cannon shots were shattering the armor on the *Carondelet*, while all the enemy shots that hit the armor of the *Arkansas* were deflected because of the slant

The Federal gunboat Carondelet. Though a veteran of Fort Henry, Fort Donelson, and Island No. 10, the Carondelet was the first victim of the Arkansas.

of her casemate. Brown himself wrote later of this stage in the fight, "While our shot seemed always to hit his stern and disappear, his missiles, striking our ironclad shield, were deflected over my head and lost in the air."

The captain of the *Carondelet* saw the contest was unequal, so he turned back, followed by the other two boats. Brown pursued as fast as he could, following a zigzag course because of the vulnerability of his bow armor. As he closed in, enemy fire grew worse. One shell struck the *Arkansas'* pilot house, killing the pilot and disabling his assistant. A plucky sailor volunteered to try to steer the boat. Brown himself was stunned by one shell, and then grazed on the temple by a minie ball. He was incapacitated for a brief time, while the *Arkansas* closed in on the *Carondelet*.

When Captain Brown returned to action, he found the *Carondelet* disabled from loss of her steering mechanism. Soon the warship became mired in the shallows and started listing. Brown steamed as close to her as he could and gave her a full broadside that made the *Carondelet* almost roll over. The men gave three hearty cheers at seeing their hearty opponent so disabled, and Brown set after the two other Union boats. They, however, were altogether lighter and quicker than the *Arkansas* and made good their escape.

Loading a powerful cannon on a gunboat was no easy task, especially during battle.

The Arkansas in a grueling battle with the Carondelet. Taking the worst of the conflict, the Carondelet was seriously disabled while the Arkansas proceeded downstream to engage Farragut.

The War Eagle

The Civil War saw a variety of regimental mascots ranging from dogs and cats to bears, raccoons, wildcats, and gamecocks. Many of these were simply pets kept in camp by homesick soldiers. Only a few actually accompanied their owners into battle. Being a mascot could be a truly hazardous occupation, as is attested by the example of Sallie the "war dog," mascot of the 11th Pennsylvania Infantry. Sallie followed her owners for 46 months, even producing a few puppies in camp. She did not shirk from entering battle, and survived Gettysburg only to be felled at the battle of Hatcher's Run on 6 February 1865.

Most famous of all Civil War regimental mascots was "Old Abe" the war eagle, mascot of the 8th Wisconsin Infantry. Abe was hatched in early 1861 and became an orphan when a Chippewa Indian killed his mother and captured Abe by cutting down the tree that held his nest. The Indian sold his eaglet to a family named McCann, who attempted to raise the bird as a pet. The eagle tolerated human company, but soon became too big and too wild to remain tethered. This disposition led the McCanns to part with their eagle, which they sold for $2.50 to a group of newly enlisted Union soldiers who called themselves the "Eau Claire Badgers."

The Eau Claire Badgers were ordered in September 1861 to report to Camp Randall in Madison, where they were enrolled as Company C of the 8th Wisconsin Infantry. The Badgers brought their newly acquired pet eagle along with them. Much to everyone's delight, the bird thrived on martial music during parades. At one time he even left his perch to stretch his wings and grab the tip of the company's flag, an event noted by the troops as well as the local newspapers.

Old Abe (named reverently after President Abe Lincoln) served with Company C of the 8th throughout the war. He was kept on a special perch, and guarded by select troops (color guards), who also protected the regiment's flags. Abe was even carried regularly into battle—36 times in all, including Corinth, Vicksburg, and Pleasant Hill. Reportedly he would fly from his perch during combat and yell and screech to encourage his owners to valor. (More recent interpretations suggest that the poor bird may have instead been screeching out of fear and attempts to escape the din of combat). Abe's antics in battle brought notoriety to the 8th, which soon became known as the Eagle Regiment. Some Confederate soldiers offered a reward to whoever could capture or kill Old Abe, while others derisively called him "Old Goose" or "Yankee Crow."

Abe was never wounded in battle, but suffered several close calls. One came at the battle of Corinth, Mississippi, in October 1862. His tether was broken by enemy fire, and he attempted to fly off. He ran off only about 50 feet and was recaptured by one of his guards before becoming airborne. After that his wings were clipped to prevent his ever flying off again.

Another close call came during the great assault on Vicksburg of 22 May 1863, when the 8th was ordered to attack Vicksburg's northern defenses along the Graveyard Road. The regiment met such heavy enemy fire that the unit had to dive for cover after suffering heavy casualties. At this time Abe had to be forcibly held down, at least until his attention was diverted by a rabbit one of the soldiers found and offered him for a snack.

As the war went on, Abe gained more and more fame and notoriety. Often tourists and even generals came to camp just to see him. Abe apparently enjoyed his role as spoiled mascot thoroughly. He always had the run of the camp, and often stole bits of food (even shots of liquor) whenever he wanted.

After the war ended, Abe returned to Wisconsin and remained quite a celebrity. For several years he was exhibited at fund raising affairs for veterans groups and orphanages. When not on tour, he was kept in a special room in the basement of the Capitol building in Madison. One of his greatest triumphs was at the 1876 Wisconsin Centennial Exposition. He was trained to give his "autograph" by poking a hole in his photograph with his beak.

In his later years, Abe regularly had a special keeper assigned to care for him—often a crippled soldier. He died on 25 March 1881, from the effects of smoke inhaled during a basement fire near his quarters in the Capitol. The dead hero's body was then stuffed and preserved, only to be lost in another fire in 1904. Today Abe the war eagle is honored by a 6 foot tall bronze statue atop the Wisconsin monument at Vicksburg, dedicated 22 May 1911. (The original statue was struck by lightning in the 1940s, and has been replaced.)

Brown now entered the main channel of the Mississippi and found himself face to face with the Union fleet of almost 40 warships—"a forest of masts and smokestacks, sloops, rams, ironclads and other gunboats on the left side, and ordinary river steamboats and bomb-vessels on the right." Brown deeply regretted that he was not able to employ his ship as a ram, for he could have had a field day against the wooden Union warships. Reports from his engine room showed that his steam pressure was dangerously low after the morning fight (down from 120 pounds to 20), so Brown did not think he would have enough power to ram anyone successfully.

Brown boldly plunged into the midst of the Union fleet, aiming his course towards Farragut's flagship, the *Hartford*. His armament took a severe pounding and temperatures in the engine room reached 120 degrees, but he pressed on, giving much more damage than he was taking. The attack was aided by the element of surprise, and the fact that the great number of Union ships limited the room available in which to maneuver. In addition, Brown was able to keep all his guns in action and still be certain of hitting targets. Each Yankee ship, on the other hand, was able to bring only a few guns to bear at a time, and any shots that missed the *Arkansas* were likely to strike another Union ship nearby.

During the fighting, the *Arkansas* caused serious damage to the *Hartford*, the *Iroquois*, and the *Benton*. Brown was aware that the greatest danger to him was posed by the Union rams, which darted at him whenever the opportunity arose. The one that came closest was the *Lancaster*, stopped by a lucky shot through her boilers that released all her steam. Crew members had to jump into the water to escape being scalded, and the *Lancaster* drifted harmlessly away.

By now the *Arkansas*' course and the current of the river had carried her through the Union fleet. The Northern boats were still buzzing like bees, and Farragut himself was furious that a makeshift enemy ironclad had sailed at will right through his fleet. Brown's boat was in no condition to renew the fight—men were bloodied and exhausted, the smokestack was full of holes, a portion of armor plating had been knocked loose, and fuel was almost gone. Brown had no choice, but to proceed the short distance to Vicksburg for repairs. There he was greeted with great jubilation at the docks. This joy, though, was tempered by close-up examination of the battered boat and its casualties: "a great heap of mangled and ghastly slain lay on the gun deck, with rivulets of blood running away from them. There was a poor fellow torn asunder, another mashed flat, whilst in the 'slaughter house' (gun deck) brains, hair and blood were all about."

Farragut, his fighting blood now boiling, decided he had had enough of being stranded upstream of Vicksburg and dealing with ebbing water and ironclads. Impulsively, he decided to run his fleet past Vicksburg a second time, to return to the downstream side of the fortress. In the process he hoped also to corner and sink the pesky *Arkansas*.

Farragut's attack began just before sunset. Once again the sky above Vicksburg was filled with thunder and shrieking shells as the shore batteries and Yankee boats exchanged blasts. And Captain Brown was not one to turn down a good fight, as beat-up as his boat was. Just as he was preparing to move out, a shell plowed into his engine room, so rendering the *Arkansas* immobile. Brown had to spend the entire battle anchored at shore, able to blast away only one broadside. It was probably just as well for him to be stuck there, since his weakened craft probably would not have been able to withstand a third battle that day.

A combination of other favorable factors also saved the *Arkansas* that evening. Since she had been painted a brownish color, it was difficult for the Yankees to see her huddled under the riverbank. Had she been seen, she surely would have been rammed. But the river current carried Farragut's boats past faster than they expected. Farragut succeeded in bringing his fleet past the city, leaving the *Arkansas* safely behind.

The Arkansas easily glides through the Federal fleet outside of Vicksburg.

Farragut was still furious at the *Arkansas*, and devised yet another plan to sink her. At dawn on 22 July he and Commander Davis sent two boats, the *Essex* and the *Queen of the West* to ram the pesky ironclad. Brown was ready for the fight, even though he had aboard only a greatly reduced crew of fewer than 40 men. These brave men fired their guns as fast as they could, slowing the Union rams considerably. Still the *Essex* came on, striking a sharp blow that was supported by a well aimed broadside that disabled almost half of Brown's reduced crew. Brown himself later wrote that the *Essex* might have sunk the *Arkansas* had she come at her with the river current rather than across it. The Yankees also could have captured the *Arkansas* had they realized the small size of her crew and put ashore a landing party. As it was, the two ships broke apart, and the *Essex* drifted downstream. The *Queen of the West* could then have dealt the *Arkansas* a mortal blow, but the captain maintained his approach and dealt Brown's boat a glancing blow. Thus the battle ended with the *Arkansas* again triumphant.

Farragut had had enough of the whole situation. The *Arkansas* was too tough to crack, his boats were unable to take Vicksburg without significant army support, and the river level was dropping daily. On 24 July, under orders from Washington, he sailed south with all his warships but two, which were ordered to keep an eye on the *Arkansas*. Four days later Commander Davis took his small flotilla north to Helena, Arkansas. Vicksburg was finally free of its enemy attackers, and everybody contributed the success to Captain Brown and the *Arkansas*.

Captain Brown was exhausted from his two months of strenuous effort finishing the *Arkansas* and then fighting the enemy. He left orders for his boat to be repaired, and then went on leave to rest up with friends in Grenada, Mississippi. At Grenada he fell ill and had to stay longer than planned. During his absence, General Earl Van Dorn ordered the *Arkansas* to head south and assist General John Breckinridge in a campaign to retake Baton Rouge. Because Breckinridge needed the boat by 5 August, there was no time to wait for Brown's return to duty. His next in command, Lieutenant Stevens, took the *Arkansas* south. Brown was furious about being left behind, since he knew he was the only one who understood the boat's workings completely. Brown's fears proved true, Stevens pushed the boat's engines too hard, and she broke down and drifted ashore about five miles south of Baton Rouge in full sight of the enemy. The proud warship was unable to move or fire a shot as a Union ram bore down on her. Lieutenant Stevens had no choice but to order his crew to abandon ship. Then, with tears in his eyes, he set the boat afire and she went to pieces in a series of mighty explosions. Thus the greatest of the Confederate ironclads passed into history—"with colors flying, the gallant *Arkansas*, whose decks had never been pressed by the foot of an enemy, was blown into the air."

One of the vessels sent to sink the Arkansas, the Essex.

CHAPTER V

GRANT TAKES COMMAND

The withdrawal of the Union fleet from Vicksburg and the loss of the *Arkansas* closed the first phase of Union operations against Vicksburg. The navy had tried for three months to take the town, but was unable to do so with its guns alone. Future efforts to take the town were directed from the landward side, and organized by Major General U.S. Grant, who put his career on the line against the "Gibraltar of the West."

Grant's career had been put temporarily on hold despite his victory at Shiloh in early April because of suspicions about his drinking and accusations that his laxness had permitted the Confederate surprise attack at Shiloh. Thus in the summer of 1862 he was consigned to guarding railroads in the District of West Tennessee, with his headquarters at Corinth, Mississippi. His command totaled almost 50,000 men, but they were too dispersed to enable him to assume an offensive. Grant wanted to be able to move on Vicksburg, or at least attack Vicksburg's railroad link to the east at Jackson, but he simply lacked the strength and the authorization to do so.

Thus Grant sat inactive while Farragut and the navy attempted in vain to take Vicksburg in the summer of 1862. In the fall, all attention in the West shifted from Vicksburg to Kentucky, where Confederate Generals Braxton Bragg and Kirby Smith were leading a desperate invasion. Back in Mississippi, General Earl Van Dorn decided to take advantage of this situation now that Vicksburg was free of pressure. What he wanted to do was put pressure on Grant and drive the Yankees out of Mississippi. In order to accomplish this, he needed to unite whatever field forces he could spare with the 16,000 man force commanded by Major General Sterling Price, which was in eastern Mississippi.

Ulysses S. Grant before the Vicksburg Campaign.

When Van Dorn had difficulty concentrating his command, Price decided to move forward on his own. He occupied Iuka on 13 September, and set about looking for Major General William S. Rosecrans' Union command, which was operating somewhere between Iuka and Corinth, located about 30 miles to the northwest of Iuka.

U.S. Grant

U.S. Grant, the greatest Union general of the war, did not have the looks or bearing of a soldier. He was under average height, and had plain brown hair and blue eyes. He did not care much for dress, and even as Union commander-in-chief wore what was comfortable rather than regulation. Given his nature and weaknesses, it was surprising that he managed to rise to army command and hold it, especially after his near disaster at Shiloh. It was his strengths that brought him to Lincoln's attention—he was a doer, a man of action, and a master strategist. These were the traits most evident in his significant victory at Vicksburg, a victory that led him on to other, equally great victories at Chattanooga and in Virginia.

Grant's life, however, was not always full of success. He was born in Point Pleasant, Ohio, in 1822, the son of a hardworking tanner. Since young Grant was not interested in the tanning business, his father obtained for him an appointment to West Point. It is interesting to note that the Congressman who entered Grant's application mistakenly wrote his name as "Ulysses Simpson Grant" rather than his given name of "Hiram Ulysses Grant." The future general, who never much cared for the name "Hiram" anyway, willingly accepted the new name "Ulysses Simpson" (Simpson was his mother's maiden name). Thus he became "U.S.Grant," initials that were popularized by the national press when he obtained the unconditional surrender of Fort Donelson in February 1862.

Grant's best subjects at West Point were math, engineering, and horsemanship. He did only adequately in his other subjects, but still managed to graduate 21st of the 39 cadets in the class of 1843. He was then assigned to the 4th U.S. Infantry as a lieutenant. His Mexican War service with Winfield Scott earned him a promotion to captain, but he did not win as much distinction in the war as did many of his fellows.

Grant's postwar service took him to a series of boring garrison posts that included Detroit, Washington state, and California. He became lonesome for his wife Julia Dent (whom he had married in 1848) and his children, and took to heavy drinking in California. This led to some sort of scandal which is still not fully understood today. Because of it he had to resign from the army in 1854.

Grant then returned to private life, but had extreme difficulty earning a satisfactory living. From 1854 to 1858 he ran a farm (Hardscrabble) given to him by his father-in-law. When this did not suit him, he moved to St. Louis and tried his hand at real estate. His lack of business sense caused him to fail at this work, so in 1860 he moved to Galena, Illinois, to work in his father's leather store.

It is as field commander in the army that Grant found his true calling. He was appointed colonel of the 21st Illinois, and unexpectedly won promotion to brigadier general because of the political backing of Illinois Congressman Elihu Washburne. Another piece of good luck came when he was appointed command of the District of Southern Illinois headquartered at Cairo. Here he was in perfect position to lead the Union drive down the Mississippi.

In November 1861 Grant led an attack on the Confederate forces at Belmont, Missouri. Though the battle was a draw, he won the attention of his superiors for his aggressiveness. After Belmont, Grant formed a firm friendship with Admiral Andrew H. Foote. The two officers cooperated very well in the campaign against Forts Henry and Donelson (February 1862), which won Grant national attention. This favor was almost lost when his army was surprised at Shiloh on 6 April. Grant redeemed his fighting reputation by winning the battle on 7 April, but remained under suspicion for drinking and related problems.

It was the Vicksburg campaign that showed Grant's determination and grasp of strategy. For over six months he struggled to get at Vicksburg, which was proving a tough nut indeed to crack. He was not discouraged by defeat, until finally he hit on the brilliant plan of crossing the Mississippi south of Vicksburg and then advancing on the town from the east. He then successfully besieged the fortress while holding off Forrest's cavalry and Johnston's growing army at Vicksburg.

After Vicksburg, Grant was sent to Chattanooga, where he found Rosecrans' dispirited army under siege. Grant arrived there in mid-October, and promptly replaced Rosecrans with Thomas, the "Rock of Chickamauga." (Grant was an excellent judge of generalship, and was the main power behind Sherman's rise as general. Grant could also work reasonably well with all sorts of personalities, including George G. Meade and Ben Butler. About the only general he could not stomach was his rival from Illinois, John McClernand.)

Within a week of his arrival in Chattanooga, Grant opened up the "Cracker line" to feed the hungry troops. A month later, in late November, he broke the siege at the battle of Lookout Mountain and then drove Bragg's army off with his victory at Missionary Ridge.

Grant's spectacular success at Chattanooga convinced President Lincoln that this was the man who would win the war. Lincoln was right. Grant was appointed general in chief in March 1864, and immediately developed a plan to press the Confederacy on all fronts. Leaving his friend Sherman the job of taking Atlanta, Grant came to Virginia to personally supervise the campaign against Robert E. Lee. It took over a year of bloody fighting, including defeats at Spotsylvania and Cold Harbor, but Grant and his strategy at last emerged triumphant.

Grant was now at the pinnacle of his career, but was not prepared for all the important postwar positions that his military success and fame thrust on him. After the war he remained general in chief of the Union armies, and thus had a major role in Reconstruction when Congress decided to keep a military occupation of the South. In 1868 Grant consented to become secretary of war to replace Edwin M. Stanton, who had been fired by President Andrew Johnson.

Grant now ran for president against the Democratic candidate Horatio Seymour of New York. The general's wartime popularity and manipulated Black votes from the South enabled him to eke out a narrow popular vote victory, 3,000,000 to 2,700,000 (the electoral vote was not as close: 214 to 80). Grant's political inexperience made it difficult to deal with Congress or understand financial policy. In addition, his friends took advantage of him to promote their personal interests in what is seen today as one of the most corrupt administrations the country has ever had.

When he retired from the presidency in 1877, Grant toured the world to gain the accolades he could no longer get at home. In 1880 he declined pressure to run for a third term as president. The general then fell upon financial hard times when his friend and business advisor Ferdinand Ward lost or stole all his money in 1884. Grant was embarrassed and broke, and had to turn to writing to support himself and his family. At this he proved to be quite successful, especially in his acclaimed autobiography, which he finished in 1885 only a few days before he died of throat cancer (which he probably contracted by smoking too many of the cigars he was famous for). He is buried with his wife in a magnificent tomb in upper Manhattan, New York, that is modeled after the Mausoleum in Halicarnassus, Turkey.

Van Dorn had gathered most of his command at Holly Springs, after leaving small garrisons at Vicksburg and Port Hudson. Grant responded by taking a large portion of his command to Bolivar, Tennessee, 35 miles north of Holly Springs, in order to keep an eye on Van Dorn. Grant left Sherman in charge at Memphis, and ordered Rosecrans to withdraw to Corinth. In order to aid Rosecrans, Grant dispatched Brigadier General E.O.C. Ord and his division, with a warning to be wary of an ambush by either Van Dorn or Price.

When Grant heard that Price was at Iuka, he changed his plan and accompanied Ord's division. His new orders were for Rosecrans and Ord to strike Price at dawn on 19 September. However, these had to be changed when Rosecrans reported that a guide had misled him and he would not be in position until 1300. Grant then directed Ord not to attack until he heard the firing from Rosecran's assault. Ord waited all day, but heard no firing, so he did nothing, assuming that Rosecrans had not begun his attack.

Confederate General who invaded Kentucky in 1862 only to be turned back at the Battle of Perryville, Braxton Bragg.

Victor at Iuka and Corinth, William S. "Rosey" Rosecrans.

Earl Van Dorn.

The Arkansas is blown up to prevent it from falling into enemy hands.

Rosecrans, meanwhile, was doing his best to carry out Grant's orders. He finally reached Price's lines at about 1600 and immediately launched his attack. The battle was hard fought, and eventually Rosecrans got the upper hand, inflicting 1,500 casualties while losing 800. The next morning Price retreated, and Grant lost his chance to isolate and destroy Price's command. Curiously, Grant and Ord had stood idle all day on the 19th within miles of Rosecrans' battle. They did not hear the noise of the battle because of the lay of the land and the direction the wind was blowing. This strange phenomenon, called "acoustic shadow," was attested several other times during the war; in some battles observers could see the fighting but not hear it because of unusual atmospheric conditions.

Grant now deemed the Confederate threat was over, and redistributed his troops to guard his assigned railways. Rosecrans remained at Corinth with 25,000 men, while Ord returned to Bolivar with 12,000; Sherman still held Memphis with 7,000, and Grant was with his strategic reserve of 6,000 at Jackson, Tennessee, 45

Slaves from Mississippi plantations flock to Federal lines in search of freedom.

miles north of Corinth. Meanwhile Van Dorn and Price finally linked up, giving them a combined command of 22,000. They thought this force would be large enough to defeat Rosecrans at Corinth, if they could achieve a surprise attack.

Rosecrans, however, received word of the Confederate movements and was prepared for their attack early on 3 October. To meet them he occupied a chain of old Confederate works located north and west of the town. Here they were struck by a much larger force than Rosecrans expected. The Union lines broke, but the Confederates were prevented from achieving total victory by the intense heat of the day and some weak generalship at the division level.

Another casualty of the battle of Corinth was Earl Van Dorn himself, who was relieved of department command because of his failures; he was transferred to a cavalry command and reappeared later in the campaign. Van Dorn's replacement was John C. Pemberton of Pennsylvania, newly promoted to the rank of lieutenant general. Pemberton had been in command at Charleston, South Carolina, but was relieved to make room for the popular P.G.T. Beauregard. This made him available at just the moment when authorities in Richmond were growing weary of Earl Van Dorn. Though Pemberton was a native Pennsylvanian, his loyalties were now solidly with the South.

Pemberton set up his headquarters in Jackson, Mississippi, on 14 October, and proceeded on to survey the defenses of his two principal posts at Vicksburg and Port Hudson. He was not very happy with the discipline of the 24,000 troops he inherited from Van Dorn, so he at once set about reorganizing and drilling them. Nor was he happy with the defensive works at Vicksburg and Port Hudson. Previous commanders had fortified only the river bluffs, leaving the landward defenses largely undeveloped. Pemberton set to work over the next four

Slaughtered in the battle of Corinth, Confederate dead lie in piles awaiting burial.

weeks to ring both towns with landward defenses to have clear fields of fire. He also fortified Snyder's Bluff at the mouth of the Yazoo River north of Vicksburg, and Warrenton six miles below Vicksburg. His efforts were praised by everyone, even the soldiers who wielded the shovels and pickaxes.

Grant, meanwhile, was reaping benefits from the twin victories at Iuka and Corinth, though he had not been personally present at either battle. Union authorities in Washington were hungry for heroes, particularly in view of their mounting list of failures in Virginia that year. As a reward for his able handling of his department, Grant on 16 October was given command of the newly created Department of Tennessee. He immediately concentrated 30,000 men of his command at Grand Junction, Tennessee, midway between Memphis and Corinth, and prepared to advance on Holly Springs. Sherman was directed to march south along the Mississippi in order to protect Grant's left flank.

The size and make-up of Sherman's command for this movement was uncertain up until the moment he departed from Memphis. It seems that Major General John McClernand, nominally one of Grant's division commanders, had been in Washington lobbying for an independent command to lead down the Mississippi to take Vicksburg. His arguments convinced Secretary of War Stanton and President Lincoln, who on 20 October gave McClernand sealed orders that stated: "When a sufficient force, not required by the operations under General Grant's command, shall be raised, an expedition may be organized under General McClernand's command against Vicksburg and to clear the Mississippi River and open navigation to New Orleans."

Grant was totally unaware of McClernand's machinations when he laid the final plans for his campaign, which he explained to Sherman personally on 15 November at Columbus, Kentucky. The movement got underway when Sherman left Memphis on 24 November with troops that McClernand had been coveting for his own use. On the 27th, Grant moved south from Grand Junction with two divisions, and Brigadier General A.P. Hovey sent a small force south from Helena to cooperate with Sherman.

Pemberton did not have enough men to oppose Grant's advance, so he withdrew his garrison from Holly Springs and concentrated his forces 20 miles to the south behind the Tallahatchie River. Grant occupied Holly Springs on 29 November, and began pushing on towards Pemberton's position. Pemberton, faced with three enemy forces advancing on a wide front (Hovey, Sherman, and Grant), was forced to withdraw again, this time to Grenada, which he occupied on 5 December.

One of the men who made the Union victorious in the Civil War, William T. Sherman.

Grant was by now becoming concerned about the length of his supply line, which stretched 180 miles all the way back to Columbus, Kentucky. He began establishing a major depot at Holly Springs. While this was being built, he hit upon a new strategy for the campaign. He would hold Pemberton's main force pinned at Grenada while Sherman advanced from Memphis to Vicksburg. When Sherman reached his goal, Grant could then deal with Pemberton at his ease.

In preparation for his new role in the campaign, Sherman now gathered over 30,000 men in Memphis. To support him, Admiral Porter (now commanding the fleet on the upper Mississippi) also gathered his forces. Preparatory for the campaign, Porter sent an expedition led by the USS *Cairo* to scout the Yazoo River. This mission ended in utter failure when the *Cairo* hit a torpedo and sank on 12 December. This disaster was a great blow to Union naval pride, and also served good notice to the Confederates that a new major enemy movement was afoot.

Grant's well laid plans began to unravel on 19 December, the very day that Sherman began his advance south from Memphis. On that day he received news that the Confederate cavalry genius Nathan B. Forrest was making havoc with his railroad supply lines in Tennessee (see sidebar). This change in affairs forced Grant to stop his forward operations against Pemberton, and look to securing his line of operations.

Grant was dealt a second, equally great blow early the next day when a large Confederate cavalry force captured and totally destroyed his supply base at Holly Springs. This force, consisting of all of Pemberton's cavalry, some 3,500 men, was commanded by none other than Major General Earl Van Dorn, Pemberton's predecessor as department commander. Van Dorn had left Grenada on 17 December with the expressed purpose of conducting a surprise raid on Holly Springs.

Van Dorn conducted his raid perfectly. He sent his troopers into Holly Springs from three directions (east, northeast, and north) while a detachment blockaded a southern road to prevent Union reinforcements from arriving. His dawn attack caught most of the 1500 Yankee defenders asleep in bed. The entire force was captured, and the Confederates set about plundering almost $2,000,000 in supplies of every description. Some troops also cut telegraph lines and tore up a long section of railroad track. The raiders carried off what they could, and then set fire to the warehouses, official buildings, and a big new hospital.

Grant was furious at this defeat, and sent all the cavalry he could (those who were not busy chasing Forrest) to try to catch Van Dorn. The wily Confederate escaped by heading north, away from Grant's main force at Oxford, Mississippi. Van Dorn threatened Union garrisons at

Location of Morgan L. Smith's division during Sherman's failed assault at Chickasaw Bluffs. Sherman lost 2000 men in the attack while inflicting negligible casualties on the Confederates.

The Saga of the *USS Cairo*

The key element needed to carry out the Union plan to conquer the Mississippi Valley was a fleet of riverine warships. At first a few steamboats were armor plated and equipped with cannons, but Union General-in-Chief Winfield Scott quickly realized that specially constructed shallow draft warships would be needed to carry out the job. Accordingly, plans were drawn up by Samuel Pook for seven special gunboats that would carry 13 cannons and two-and-one-half inches of armor plate while being able to move at nine miles an hour and have a draft of no more than six feet. In August the War Department ordered seven of these boats to be built at a cost of $100,000 each. They were called "city class" gunboats since they were to be named after ports of the Mississippi tributaries.

The contract for the construction of these gunboats was awarded to James B. Eads of Indiana, a noted inventor and mechanic. It was to be a rush job, with delivery set for October. Eads employed 4000 workmen day and night, but had to adjust the design as he progressed. Other problems delayed completion of the boats until January 1862. Although the boats were built in six months instead of the required 65 days, they were soon known as "90 day wonders." Three - the *Cairo, Mound City*, and *Cincinnati* were built at Mound City, Illinois. The other four, *St. Louis, Louisville, Carondelet*, and *Pittsburgh* were constructed at Carondelet, Missouri.

The lightest and quickest of the seven Eads gunboats was the *Cairo* (pronounced KAY-ROH). She was 175 feet long and carried 122 tons of armor with a total displacement of 600 tons. Her speed of 6 knots per hour was reached using a 22-foot paddlewheel driven by five coal burning boilers. The gunboat's armament consisted of six 32-pounders, three 42-pounders, three 8-inch Dahlgrens, and a 30-pounder Parrott rifles.

The *Cairo* was not destined to have a lucky career. She missed the fighting at Forts Henry and Donelson, where several of her sister ships played a key role in Grant's first major campaign. She did not see important action until 6 June when the *Cairo, St. Louis, Carondelet* and several lesser ships defeated the Confederate River Defense Fleet at the battle of Memphis.

The *Cairo*'s historical claim to fame came on December 12, 1862, during naval operations connected to Grant's first drive on Vicksburg. In early December two Union ironclad boats, the *Marmara* and *Signal*, scouted the Yazoo and found numerous enemy "torpedoes" placed in the river 15 to 20 miles from its mouth. These torpedoes, also known as mines, were simply five gallon glass jugs that were filled with gunpowder and set to float at or near the surface of the river. The mines were ignited by a friction tube attached to a metal wire that was pulled at the right moment by a soldier on the shore. These homemade mines were not yet tried in battle, but they appeared to pose enough of a threat to Union boats moving towards Vicksburg that Lieutenant Commander Thomas O. Selfridge was ordered to take the *Cairo* and several supporting ships to clear them out.

Selfridge's mine clearing expedition sailed up the Yazoo early on 12 December, with the *Marmara* leading the way. When the *Marmara* ran into the enemy about 1100, Selfridge, aboard the *Cairo*, hurried to her relief. Upon reaching the *Marmara*, Selfridge was unable to advance because of torpedoes in the river. He stopped his warship and launched a small boat to clear the torpedoes. As the boat was being lowered, the river's current caused the *Cairo* to begin to drift towards the shore. To correct the drift, Selfridge reversed his ship's engines. The *Cairo*'s wheels made only a few revolutions before hitting some mines.

Selfridge later described the scene: "Two sudden explosions in quick succession occurred, one close to my port quarter, the other apparently under my port bow—the latter so severe as to raise the guns under it some distance from the deck. She commenced to fill so rapidly that in two or three minutes the water was over her forecastle. I shoved her immediately for the bank, but a few yards distant . . . the *Cairo* sunk minutes after the explosion, going totally out of sight, except the top of the chimneys."

It was now about 1210. Commander Selfridge had carried out his orders all too efficiently—one wag put it, "He was ordered to remove enemy torpedoes from the river and neatly did so by placing his ship over them." Thus the *Cairo* became the first modern warship in history to be sunk by a torpedo. All poor Selfridge could do was to remove the *Cairo's* flag, which was still flying above water level, and then knock over the ship's smokestacks so the Confederates could not board the wreck.

The Union Navy thought for awhile of raising the *Cairo*, but never got around to doing so. The sunken warship then remained buried in the Yazoo river mud, undisturbed for decades except for occasional curiosity seekers who looked for souvenirs at times of low water.

In the 1950s, rumors of the *Cairo's* location began to intrigue Edwin C. Bearss, longtime historian at the Vicksburg National Military Park. He researched the location of the gunboat's sinking, and on 12 November 1956, set out with three friends in a small motorboat to try to locate the wreck. Bearss planned to use only a small compass to find the *Cairo*, figuring that the wreck's iron armament and cannons would readily attract the compass' needle. His theory proved right, and the boat's remains were quickly found.

Bearss had to wait three years before returning to investigate the wreck further. In October 1959, two divers brought up some wood and eight-inch iron spikes. Much more significant remains were recovered in 1960. Using a winch on a barge, Bearss recovered an eight-inch gun, as well as the *Cairo's* intact turret housing.

Bearss decided to try to raise the Cairo and preserve it as a naval museum. The project turned out to be a more difficult one than anticipated because of the weight of the wreck's armor, water-soaked timbers, and enveloping mud. The first attempt at raising the wreck came in 1963 when cables were attached to it from two barges. The attempt failed when the barges broke loose and snapped their cables. A new plan was then developed to run cables under the boat and then raise it up with cranes on barges. This attempt was abandoned when it was discovered that the lifting cables were cutting through the wreck's water soaked hull timbers.

Because of damage done to the wreck in the first two salvage attempts, Bearss felt that it would be impossible to raise the *Cairo* in one piece. He decided to raise the boat in three sections, fore, center, and aft. This technique worked, and the wreck's third section was raised on 12 December 1964, the 102nd anniversary of the boat's sinking. The boat's remains were then transferred to the Ingalls Shipyard in Pascagoula, Mississippi, for restoration. Work progressed over the next 12 years, but the boat's fragile timbers also suffered from the sun and more than one hurricane.

In 1977 the remains of the *Cairo* were taken to Vicksburg to be displayed in a specially designed museum structure on the battlefield. The surviving portion of the boat is fairly intact below the water line, except for the portions blown out by the explosion that sank the gunboat. These timbers have been reinforced, and additional timbers have been added to flesh out the boat's framework above the water line. Visitors today can even "walk through" the boat to get a feeling for its size. Separate exhibits show the boat's original boilers, engine machinery, guns and armor. Adjacent to the outdoor shelter covering the *Cairo* is an excellent museum housing over 100 small artifacts found in the wreck. These items have proved as historically interesting—perhaps more so—than the wreck itself. Finds such as toothbrushes, combs, pencils, mustard bottles and rubber bands have revealed a great deal about the equipment and daily life of the men who manned the *Cairo*.

The story of the wreck and salvage of the *Cairo* has been excellently told by Mr. Bearss in his book *The Hardluck Ironclad*.

The Federal gunboat Cairo. Though a formidable vessel, she was sunk by a torpedo on the Yazoo. Raised up after lying on the river bottom for almost a century, it is now on exhibit at Vicksburg National Park.

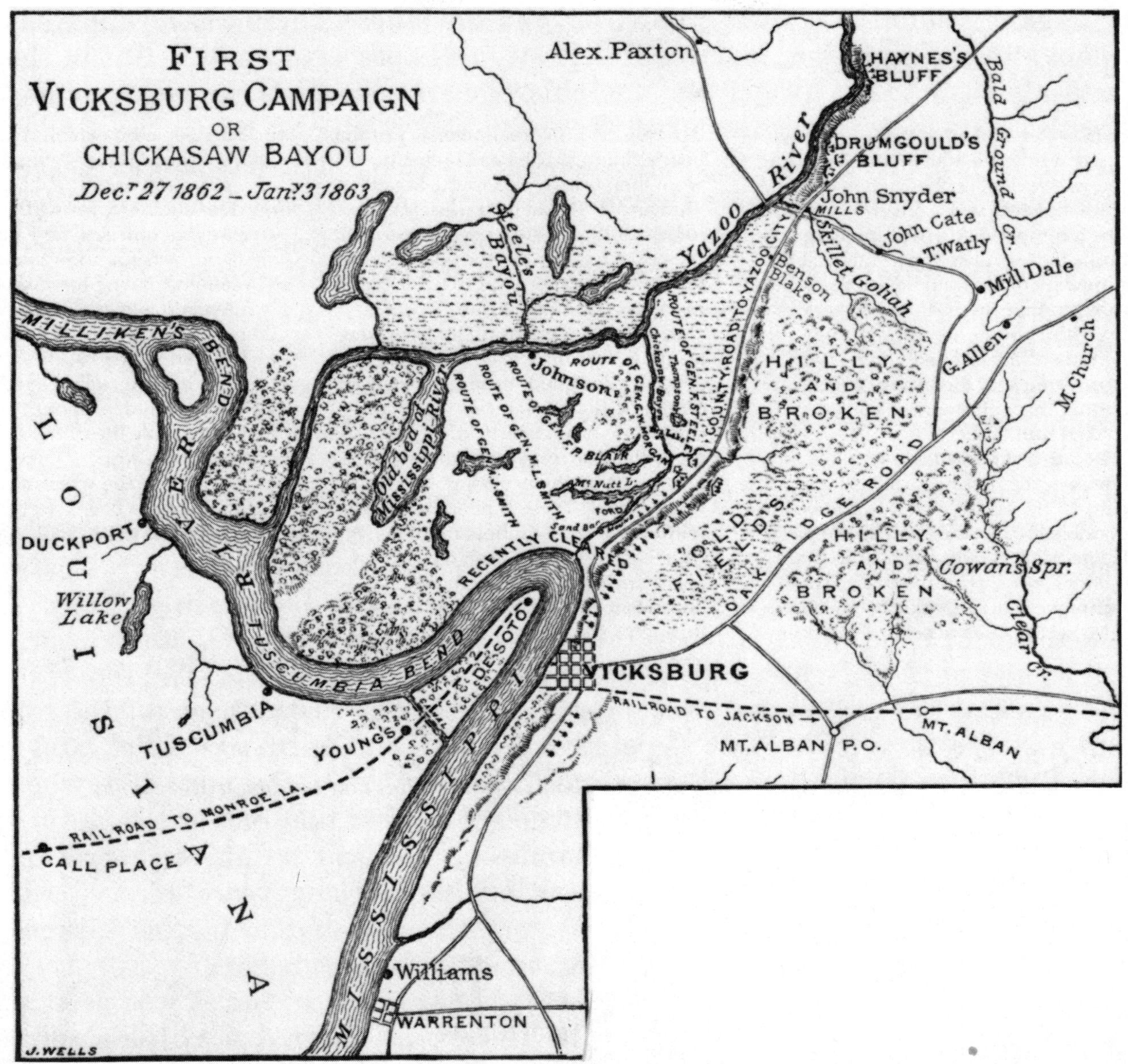

LaGrange and Bolivar, Tennessee, before returning safely to Grenada on 28 December.

Grant immediately realized that Forrest's and Van Dorn's raids had dealt a critical role to his campaign. Since Van Dorn had completely destroyed his advance supply base and Forrest had ruined his supply lines, Grant felt he had no choice but to withdraw from Mississippi. On 21 December he began retreating to Holly Springs and Grand Junction, and from there to Memphis, which he reached on 10 January.

On 23 December Grant sent a message from Holly Springs to Sherman to tell him that his supply lines had been cut and he was withdrawing. Consequently he would be unable to hold Pemberton's forces at Grenada, and Sherman should alter his plans accordingly. Unfortunately for Sherman, this note took some time to reach him because of the havoc the Confederate cavalry had caused to the Union rail and telegraphic lines. Grant's important message had to go by courier to Memphis and then by boat to Sherman's command on its way to Vicksburg. This round about route delayed it until 3 January, when Sherman finally received it via McClernand.

Sherman had left Memphis on 20 December, having organized his 20,000 men into three divisions. Accompanying him were Porter's gunboats and a fleet of 67 transports. On the 21st he reached Helena and picked up a another division of 12,000 men commanded by Brigadier General Frederick Steele. Four days later Sherman arrived at Milliken's Bend, 20 miles above Vicksburg. From there he sent A.J. Smith's division to the west bank of the river to occupy the railroad line that ran to DeSoto Point. Sherman had his remaining three divisions at the mouth of the Yazoo, where they disembarked to attack the Confederate lines.

Sherman was not totally prepared for the variety of obstacles he met when he landed on 26 December at Johnson's Plantation opposite the mouth of Steele's Bayou. From there it was a four-mile march to the Confederate positions through land that was swampy and flooded by recent rains. The approach to the enemy lines was restricted to a narrow front by the Mississippi River on the right and Thompson's Lake on the left. This created a funnel and left only a three-mile stretch of Confederate line accessible to attack. To make matters worse, Chickasaw Bayou ran right in front of almost the entire enemy position, and it was crossable in only three or four places. The Confederate works were very strongly posted atop the bluffs of the Walnut Hills. There also seemed to be many more Confederate defenders than anticipated. Sherman expected 6,000, but there seemed to be more than twice that number. He had no way of knowing that Vicksburg's garrison had been heavily reinforced by Pemberton at Grenada.

Sherman moved his men forward and tested the Confederate defenses in a seven-hour long skirmish on Sunday, 28 December. He then drew up his battle plans and called for George Morgan's and Frederick Steele's divisions to carry out the main attack on the Confederate center, supported by demonstrations on each flank. Morgan had severe reservations about the operation, especially when Sherman told him, "We will lose 5000 men before we take Vicksburg, and may as well lose them here as anywhere else." To this Morgan boldly responded, "We might lose 5,000 men, but this entire army could not carry the enemy's position in my front; the larger the force sent to the assault, the greater will be the number slaughtered."

Scene where Sherman met defeat while assaulting Vicksburg, Chickasaw Bluffs.

The Defender of Vicksburg

A strange irony of fate caused Northern born Yankee John C. Pemberton to be commanding general of the Confederate forces at Vicksburg. Pemberton was born in Philadelphia on 10 August 1814. Though a Quaker (Quakers usually practiced pacifism), he entered West Point and graduated in the middle of the class of 1837.

Pemberton's pre-Civil War army career paralleled that of many of his fellow officers. He served first in the Seminole Indian War, and then in the Mexican War, where he was commended twice. After the war, he did frontier duty against the Indians and took part in the 1857 Mormon expedition.

Though he was a Northerner, Pemberton developed close ties with the South. He was a supporter of states' rights, and had several close friends from the South while at West Point. His frequent military duty in the South also led him to become attached to Southern interests. This attachment was cemented in 1848, when he married Martha Thompson, a native of Norfolk, Virginia.

The Pennsylvanian who found himself in charge of the defense of Vicksburg, John C. Pemberton.

Pemberton was faced with a weighty decision when the war began in 1861. Should he fight for the North, where he was born and raised, or for the South, his wife's home? Winfield Scott, commander of the Northern armies, was aware that Pemberton's allegiance was wavering, and offered him a promotion to colonel if he would stay in the Union Army. Pemberton unexpectedly refused the offer and resigned from the Union army when his "adopted" state of Virginia seceded in April. The fact that the Civil War was truly a contest of brother against brother is clearly seen in the Pemberton family. Two of Pemberton's brothers enlisted in the Union Army while John Pemberton rose to very high rank in the Confederate Army.

Pemberton's loyalty to the South was not questioned initially. In two months he rose from the rank of lieutenant colonel to brigadier general. He did little of note, yet was promoted in January 1862 to the rank of major general in command of the Department of

Sherman began his preparatory artillery bombardment at 1000 on the 29th. It lasted for two hours and the infantry was ordered forward. Two brigades led the assault, DeCourcy's of Morgan's division and Blair's of Steele's division. Morgan's men suffered terribly, covering the final 300 yards of open ground in front of the enemy's lines: "The assaulting forces came under a withering and destructive fire. A passage was forced over the abatis and through the murky bayou and tangled marsh to high ground. All formations were broken; the assaulting forces were jammed together, and, with a yell of desperate determination, they rushed to the assault and were mowed down by a storm of shells, grape and canister."

Blair's attack fared no better. This is what it looked like to the defenders: "A whole brigade emerged from the woods in good order and moved gallantly forward under a heavy fire of our artillery. They advanced to within 150 yards of the pits when they broke and retreated, and soon rallied and dividing their forces sent a portion to the right, which was gallantly driven back by the 28th Louisiana and 42nd Georgia regiments with heavy loss. Their attack in front was repulsed with still greater disasters. By a handsome movement on the enemy's flank the 26th and part of the 17th Louisiana threw the enemy into inextricable confusion, and were so fortunate as to capture 4 stand of regimental colors, 21 commissioned officers, 311 non-commissioned officers and privates, and 500 stand of arms."

Altogether the gallant Yankees made five separate assaults on the Confederate center. Three

South Carolina, Georgia and Florida. Here Pemberton showed himself to be an able administrator, but not unusually inspiring or energetic. Such traits make it difficult to understand why he was again promoted in October 1862 to the rank of lieutenant general in command of the Department of Mississippi, Tennessee and East Louisiana.

Pemberton's promotion to lieutenant general may have been due solely to the backing of Confederate President Jefferson Davis. Whatever Davis' reasons were, Pemberton clearly was underqualified for such high rank and the important department he was assigned. It was his fate to try to hold Vicksburg against the determined attacks of U.S. Grant.

Pemberton managed to hold Grant off for several months, but was totally fuddled and outmaneuvered by Grant's final drive on the city in April 1863. Pemberton was further confused when he received conflicting orders as to what to do when Grant was closing in on Vicksburg. His immediate superior J.E. Johnston ordered him to evacuate the town in order to save his army, while President Davis ordered him to hold Vicksburg at all costs. Pemberton chose to follow Davis' instructions, perhaps out of loyalty and gratitude for his promotion. It was to prove a disastrous decision.

The loss of Vicksburg was a permanent stain on Pemberton's career and life. What particularly galled Southerners was the fact that Pemberton consented to surrender Vicksburg on 4 July, doubling Yankee pleasure on Independence Day. The fact of the matter was that Pemberton believed he could get easier terms from Grant by agreeing to surrender on the 4th. Whatever his reasons, this act led some Southerners to suspect Pemberton's loyalty; not a few called him a traitor because of his Northern birth. Modern historians are in agreement that all Pemberton was guilty of was being an uninspired general in a crucial campaign. He never wavered in his loyalty to the South and so is undeserving of being the Confederate scapegoat for Vicksburg.

After his surrender, Pemberton was held captive in a prison at Mackinac Island, Michigan. He was exchanged in April 1864 and available for new duty, but there was no assignment available for an officer of such high rank. Consequently, he resigned his commission as lieutenant general in May 1864. His devotion to the South is demonstrated by the fact that he consented to accept an appointment as colonel of artillery for the rest of the war—a demotion unparalleled at that level.

After the war Pemberton became a farmer near Warrenton, Virginia. Eventually he found his way back to his native Pennsylvania, where he died on 13 July 1881. He was buried in Philadelphia. Today he is remembered solely as the Pennsylvania Confederate general who lost Vicksburg.

times they made it over the parapets, and once even held on for awhile. But bravery alone was not able to carry the day. The Confederate works were too strong, and there were too few attackers to complete the job. Thayer's brigade had gotten lost as it advanced, and only committed one regiment to the attack. Lindsay's brigade on the right was unable to cross the bayou and never entered the fight. Farther to the right, M.L. Smith's division was halted when its lead regiment, the 6th Missouri, got pinned down on a very narrow approach road.

Sherman finally called off the bloody attacks between 1500 and 1600. Morgan's apprehensions had turned out correct. Sherman lost almost 2000 men that day while Confederate losses were only 187.

Sherman was nevertheless undaunted, and wanted to renew the assault the next morning. Then he changed his mind, and decided to move to attack Haynes' Bluff, five miles to the left. The movement was ordered for New Year's Eve, but there was such a fog that night that everything had to be canceled. Sherman then decided to call everything off, and ordered his men to return to the mouth of the Yazoo River on 2 January. There on 3 January he finally received Grant's 23 December message that he had turned back to Memphis. Sherman now understood why there were many more defenders on Chickasaw Bluffs than he expected. Grant's withdrawal had taken all pressure off Pemberton, and Pemberton was reinforcing the Vicksburg garrison daily. Sherman now felt lucky he had not ordered a second day of assaults, for they would have been repulsed even more bloodily.

Sherman's expedition, however, was still not over. He now found his command absorbed into McClernand's grand Army of the Mississippi (see sidebar on McClernand). On 5 January, only three days after he returned from the Chickasaw Bluffs campaign, Sherman, McClernand and Porter were on their way to attack Fort Hindman in Arkansas, which commanded the approaches to Vicksburg on the western side of the river. The force arrived on 10 January, and made an assault on the next day. The immediate results were no different than earlier—1100 Union casualties to 150 Confederate. Then the fort unexpectedly surrendered its 5000 defenders. McClernand's foray had turned into a victory, and he was ready to reap the glory for it. However, Porter and Sherman found him to be impossible to work with, and complained to Grant. By the end of January, Grant finally brought McClernand's command to an end and absorbed his troops back into his own army.

Yankees of Morgan's division slog their way through the swampy mire of Chickasaw Bayou to attack impenetrable Confederate fortifications.

The River War

The Union Navy gave up its attempts to capture Vicksburg in July 1862, when the Admiral Farragut took his fleet back to New Orleans, and a small fleet was left with Grant's army above Vicksburg. In September, Admiral David D. Porter, captor of Forts Jackson and St. Phillip at New Orleans earlier in the year, received command of the Union's squadron on the upper Mississippi. Porter accompanied Sherman on the latter's unsuccessful campaign that was repulsed at Chickasaw Bluffs in late December. He then accompanied Sherman and McClernand in the successful attack on Fort Hindman at Arkansas Post in January.

In late January Porter returned to Young's Point and decided to do something about the Confederate east-west river traffic that was running freely between Vicksburg and the opposite Louisiana shore. He hit on the idea of having one of his rams make a predawn raid on Vicksburg's docks to sink the Confederate ship *City of Vicksburg*. Colonel Charles R. Ellet's *Queen of the West* was selected to carry out the mission early on February. Ellet's boat got a late start due to paddle wheel problems, and ended up making its raid in broad daylight. Surprisingly, his boat was hit only three times before reaching Vicksburg's docks. Here he was able to deal only a glancing blow to the *City of Vicksburg* because of the awkward positioning of the Confederate boat. He did manage, however, to set the boat ablaze with lighted turpentine torches his men threw at her. Ellet's own boat then caught fire, but he managed to put it out. He then boldly headed downstream, surviving the fury of Vicksburg's batteries. The *Queen of the West* received another twelve hits but could still function.

Confederates capture the ram Queen of the West after the vessel was run aground and rendered helpless.

Ellet now sailed his boat to the mouth of the Red River, and then headed back towards Vicksburg. On her cruise she destroyed three Confederate steamers. Within the next few days she received a new supply of fuel, a barge of coal that Porter let float down to him from Milliken's Bend. Ellet was now able to begin a new cruise on 10 February. He made several significant captures including one steamer with 4500 bushels of corn. These successes led him to venture farther afield, until the "Queen of the West" hit a mudbar and was captured. Ellet and most of his crew escaped on a captured steamer but had to leave the *Queen* behind.

Grant, unaware of the loss of the *Queen of the West*, sent his biggest gunboat, the *Indianola*, to aid Ellet on the 13th. The warship successfully passed the Vicksburg and Warenton batteries, only to run into a disheveled Ellet who reported his defeat. Ellet returned to friendly lines on the Louisiana shore, while the *Indianola* cruised the Mississippi.

Meanwhile, the enterprising Confederates managed to raise and refit the *Queen of the West*. The *Queen* then joined up with another warship, the *Welsh*, and several cottonclads to take care of the *Indianola*. The decisive fight took place on the night of 24 February. Because of the darkness, the *Indianola's* gunners could not aim their weapons. This gave an advantage to the Confederates, who rammed the *Indianola* three times and gave her a mortal blow. Her captain had no choice but to head her into the bank. She was the second of the North's prize inland warships to be lost, following the *Cairo's* demise on the Yazoo River in December 1862.

There followed one of the strangest episodes in American naval history. Admiral Porter was not willing to let the Confederates salvage and equip the half submerged *Indianola*, so he devised a fake monster ironclad to scare the Confederates into abandoning her. The sham boat was made using a flatboat, pointed logs, canvass, fake wooden guns, two old lifeboats, and a lot of paint. Dummy paddle wheel housings were fashioned, and two fake smokestacks were made of empty pork barrels. When finished, the monster "ironclad" was 300 feet long. Its construction bill ran to $8.63. The behemoth had no name, but carried a Jolly Roger flag and the curious phrase DECIDED PEOPLE CAVE IN painted on her fake paddle wheel housings.

The fake warship was towed to midriver late on 25 February, and fires were lit in a temporary furnace. Shortly after midnight, she was set free in the river, carrying no crew. Her course and the smoke belching from her smo-

Running the batteries at Vicksburg, the Indianola presses down the Mississippi to join the Queen of the West in harassing Confederate river traffic.

kestacks did a good job convincing the Confederates she was the real item. The Southerners opened fire on the fake ship, but she just continued downstream without firing a shot in reply, carried only by the current of the river. Once past Vicksburg, the boat drifted to the Louisiana shore, where some friendly hands sent her on her way again after several hours of pushing.

The fake boat, with her smokestacks still belching, now drifted on carried by the current. She soon drew near the Confederate *Queen of the West*, which turned south in panic rather than face the monster Union warship. The master of the *Queen* rushed to the work crew tending the *Indianola*, and warned them of the great Union ironclad bearing down on them. The leader of the work crew fell for the story, and blew up the *Indianola*. They did not realize their mistake until next day, when the fake boat was discovered stranded on the river bank twelve miles upstream from the sunken *Indianola*. A brave Confederate crew rowed up to the deserted craft and were totally amazed to find it an empty wooden shell.

The loss of the *Indianola* convinced Admiral Farragut at New Orleans that it was time for him to return to Vicksburg. He fully understood that such a move would necessitate running by the strong enemy batteries at Port Hudson. He would make the run with four warships, each partially shielded from the Confederate batteries by a gunboat steaming to the starboard side.

The movement began at 2200 on 12 March and was only a mild success. Just one of the four warships, Farragut's flagship the *Hartford*, made it through relatively unscathed. She had the advantage of going first, before the Confederate batteries got the range down. Two Union warships were disabled in the fight. The *Monongahela* received a shot in her rudder and was grounded for awhile, but she was finally pulled loose by her shepherding gunboat and sent in the right direction upstream. The *Richmond* was not so lucky. She was struck by a shot in her engineroom, and had to turn back. The least lucky warship of all was the *Mississippi*, which grounded on a bend in the river; she was evacuated and set afire by her crew. Farragut used the few ships that made it past Port Hudson to run a successful blockade of the mouth of the Red River.

The river war was now quiet for the next two months. Porter's participation in the Yazoo Pass expedition in early March has been discussed elsewhere.

On 30 March a windstorm blew the Confederate ship *Vicksburg* loose from

Frightened by a Federal dummy ironclad (l), the Confederates blow up their captured prize the Indianola while the Queen of the West flees for safety.

the docks where she was being repaired for the damage received two months earlier from the *Queen of the West*. She drifted ashore a ways down stream near the *Hartford*. Before the Yankees could grab her, she was reached and burned by a Confederate squad sent out in a rowboat.

On 16 April, Porter brought most of his fleet south past Vicksburg in order to give support to Grant's planned crossing of the river later in the month. He conducted a great bombardment of the Confederate batteries at Port Hudson from 0700 to 1300 on 29 April, but was unable to silence them.

The last notable naval action of the campaign occurred on 27 May, when Porter sent five warships out at Grant's request to try to enfilade the northern defenses of Vicksburg. During this attack the gunboat *Cincinnati* was hit amidships several times by plunging fire from the Confederate heavy guns high on the river bluffs. With her pilot house and tiller shot away, she became a total wreck and sank in three fathoms of water within sight of the Confederate batteries. At least one of the fatal shots reportedly came from the Confederate cannon known as "Whistling Dick".

For the rest of the siege Porter's warships and mortar boats rendered good service keeping Grant's supply lines and communications open, and assisting in bombardments of the city. But Porter was chastened by the loss of the *Cincinnati*, and never again sent his warships in a direct attack on the Confederate works.

The Monongahela, a wooden steamer of Farragut's fleet that ran aground under fire from the Port Hudson batteries. Fortunately, the vessel was pulled free before it could be seriously damaged.

CHAPTER VI

GRANT THE RELENTLESS

At the end of January Grant concentrated his whole army on the west bank of the Mississippi north of Vicksburg. He now had some 60,000 men divided into three corps—the 13th under quarrelsome McClernand, who was angry over his demotion from army command; the 15th under Sherman, Grant's righthand man; and the 17th, under dependable Major General James B. McPherson. Grant also had available another corps, the 16th, commanded by Major General Stephen Hurlbut, who was guarding railroads in Tennessee. This force seemed large enough to take Vicksburg, but Grant first had to find a vulnerable spot to attack. Grant was persistent enough to keep trying, even though Vicksburg was to prove difficult to conquer.

Grant's other enemy, the swampy terrain above and around Vicksburg, precluded a direct assault.

Grant's Canal

Grant's first project was to complete the canal across DeSoto Point begun by General Williams the previous summer. The project seemed on paper to be a good idea, since it would bypass Vicksburg's fortifications and give Grant access to the more open terrain south of the town. Engineers thought that all the old canal needed was a little widening and deepening, and the swollen winter waters of the Mississippi would take care of the rest. The only alteration in the canal they planned to make was to angle its northern mouth more to the west in line with the direction of the river's current.

Grant assigned about 1,000 troops a day to dig the canal, supported by black slaves impressed from local plantations. Because of the mushy ground, the troops were wet all the time and most had to live aboard river transports. The men did not enjoy the muddy job, which seemed endless. Their morale was further decreased when a smallpox epidemic broke out. Sherman complained that the rising river water threatened to drown the diggers. Admiral Porter sarcastically observed that if the rains continued, the whole west bank would be flooded and his gunboats could sail over the fields wherever they wished.

Work on the canal was speeded up in February when four dredge boats arrived from Louisville. Grant, however, began to despair of the canal's usefulness, though he maintained an outward optimism. He realized that the Confederates could post guns to control the southern outlet of the canal. They had also erected strong fortifications at Warrenton, immediately south of Vicksburg, which controlled the crossings of the Big Black River. Suddenly, the idea of an attack on Vicksburg's southern defenses did not seem as attractive as before.

Sylvanus Cadwallader, a reporter for the *Chicago Times*, was even more

Where the great campaign took place, map of the general vicinity around Vicksburg.

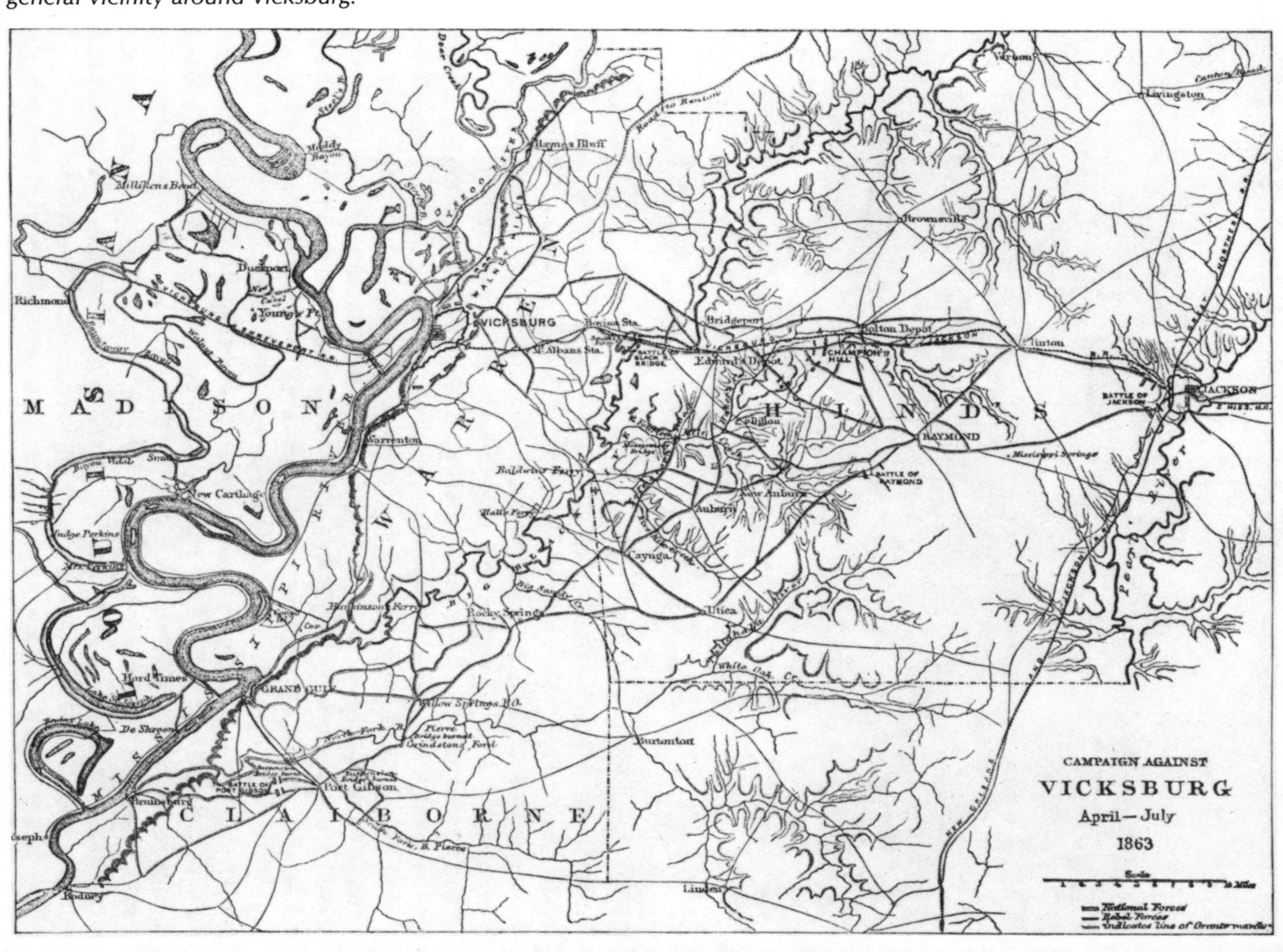

pessimistic than Grant about the project. When work was begun, he noted that the canal "was standing full of still water, without any current whatever and quite as much inclined to empty itself into the river above Vicksburg as below it." Later he observed that the work "was pressed forward with all the force that could work on it, until the rise of the river, which came soon after, did actually overflow about all of Young's Point and rendered its further prosecution impossible. It had been so nearly completed that one or two light drift vessels had traversed nearly its entire length. Our delay in completing the work had been so great that the Confederates had planted batteries on the opposite shore exactly opposite its mouth by which an enfilading fire could destroy vessels in the lower two-thirds of its length."

The flooding mentioned by Cadwallader occurred on 7 March. The work continued for a couple more weeks using dredge boats, but these had to cease operations when they came in range of the Confederate batteries at Warrenton. Thus the whole canal scheme was abandoned as a failure in mid-March.

The course of Grant's canal was visible for a long time after the war, and is still traceable today. Curiously, the DeSoto Peninsula was later cut off by nature when all human efforts to do so had failed. In the years after the war, the river's current gradually eroded away the shore of the peninsula. On 27 April 1876, water broke through, taking the main channel of the Mississippi in a new route across what had been the DeSoto Peninsula. As a result, Vicksburg today no longer sits on the Mississippi River, but on a cut off bend now.

Crane cutting away at the dam blocking the canal on the Desoto Peninsula. When all was said and done, the plan for the canal ended in complete failure.

Grant's Federals working on the Desoto Peninsula canal. The reasoning behind the construction was to allow Grant's army to bypass the Vicksburg batteries.

The Lake Providence Expedition

Because of the slow progress and limited prospects of the canal, Grant began looking for another route to get past Vicksburg on the west bank. The most attractive route appeared to run from Lake Providence, some 30 miles north of Vicksburg, south through the Tensas, Black and Red Rivers to a point 60 miles south of Vicksburg, just upstream from Port Hudson. Development of this 200-mile route involved some digging and a great deal of brush and tree clearing, but it did seem promising. Grant accordingly assigned the project to Major General James B. McPherson and his 17th Corps.

McPherson undertook the challenge energetically. His first survey of the route showed that his greatest problem would be to clear the rivers and bayous of sunken logs and stumps. For this purpose his engineers contrived a special large circular saw mounted on a platform. It could be raised or lowered depending on the depth of the underwater logs that needed cutting up. The machine worked well, but progress was slow, especially through the cypress swamp euphemistically called Bayou Baxter.

Progress advanced far enough by 8 March for McPherson to cut the northern levee above Bayou Baxter to let the Mississippi river water in to scour out the channel. Everything proceeded as anticipated when the levee was cut, though several weeks more of work were needed to clear stumps and deepen the channel. By this time Grant began to worry about what would happen when the summer heat caused the river level to ebb. For this and other reasons he stopped work on the Lake Providence project in favor of other plans.

Troops of McPherson's corps working to cut the levee at Bayou Baxter.

The Yazoo Pass Expedition

Some of Grant's staff felt that the easiest way to approach Vicksburg by water would be to sail down the Yazoo River and its tributaries, the Tallahatchie and Coldwater Rivers. The Yazoo emptied into the Mississippi just above Vicksburg at the spot where Sherman had landed prior to his attack on the Chickasaw Bluffs in December. The northern reaches of the Yazoo system had, until a few years before the war, been connected to the Mississippi by a 14-mile-long bayou called the Yazoo Pass, which emptied into the Mississippi 6 miles below Helena, Arkansas. In 1857, the state of Mississippi had sealed off the Yazoo Pass with a great dike, 100 feet wide and 6 feet high, in order to prevent the Father of Waters from flooding the fertile farmlands of the interior. Some of Grant's engineers figured it would be but a simple task to break open this dike and open up the Yazoo Pass and River for Union shipping.

On 1 February, Grant sent Lieutenant Colonel James H. Wilson of his staff to open up the dike. Accompanying him were 4,500 men under Brigadier General Leonard Ross and a flotilla of ten boats under Lieutenant Commander Watson Smith. Watson successfully planted explosives in the dike, and on 3 February blasted a hole in it that became 80 feet wide as the waters rushed through. Since the Mis-

sissippi was 8 feet higher than the level of water in the Pass, it took four days for the water levels in the two rivers to come to an equal level.

When the torrent in the Pass subsided, the Union boats entered only to find it full of snags and logs. This congestion was increased by a small force of Confederates who felled a great number of trees from nearby forests and rolled them into the Pass. It took the Yankees over two weeks to clean the Pass for navigation, and they did not reach the Coldwater River until 28 February. Grant was excited when he heard of this progress, and ordered General Ross to proceed south and see how far he could get. If things went well, Grant was prepared to send most of his army up this route.

A shallow draft "tinclad", the Marmora. Light vessels such as these were very useful cruising the shallow bayous and tributaries of the Mississippi.

Pemberton was well aware of the progress being made at the Yazoo Pass, and was prepared to meet it. He had posted Major General W.W. Loring with 20,000 men at Grenada to protect the northern approaches to Vicksburg. In mid-February, he directed Loring to proceed to the juncture of the Yazoo and Yalabusha Rivers and fortify that point against the Union forces. Loring's advance reached Greenwood on 21 February, and construction was soon started on Fort Pemberton about five miles below the mouth of the Yalabusha. By 10 March the fort was basically finished, manned by eight cannons and 2,000 men.

Ross's Union command of 4,000 men began arriving opposite Fort Pemberton on 11 March. Because of flooded ground, Ross was able to attack the fort with only a couple batteries and his light gunboats. This bombardment proved ineffectual, so Ross headed back up the river.

On his way back upstream, Ross met a brigade of reinforcements led by Brigadier General Isaac Quinby; Quinby's advance had been held up by lack of transport. As senior officer, Quinby took charge of their combined forces and directed Ross to accompany him back to Fort Pemberton. The Unionists arrived on 23 March. Quinby soon realized he did not have enough cannon power to reduce the fort, so he set about trying to find a place to land his troops. He decided he needed pontoons to do so, so he sent back to Helena for some on 27 March.

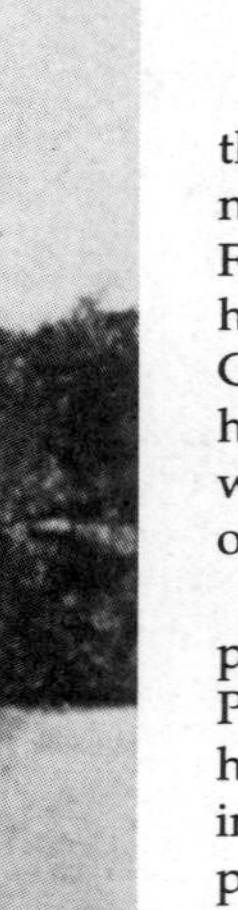

One of the gunboats that Porter took with him up the Yazoo River, the Pittsburg.

The Steele's Bayou Expedition

During Ross' attack on Fort Pemberton, Grant received word of Confederate reinforcements being sent there from Vicksburg. This caused him to fear that Ross might be surrounded and overwhelmed. In order to get help to Ross, Grant scouted an alternative inland water route that began in the Yazoo River opposite Haynes' Bluff and then proceeded north up Steele's Bayou to Cypress Lake, Black Bayou, Deer Creek, and Rolling Fork, which would bring him to the Sunflower River about 25 miles west of Greenwood and Fort Pemberton. If the route worked to send aid to Ross, it might also be useful to help turn the Vicksburg defenses.

On 16 March, Grant ordered Sherman to take part of the 15th Corps and proceed up Steele's Bayou, accompanied by Admiral Porter with five ironclads, four mortar boats, and two tugs. Progress was extremely slow because of floating debris and logs that held the ironclads' progress to four miles in 24 hours. Sherman's infantry had to be shuttled forward using the two tugboats. As the task force proceeded farther north, it ran into enemy sniper fire. Progress became even slower when the Confederates began to fell trees across the channel. When they blocked the channel with a sunken coal barge, Porter knew he was in for trouble, particularly when he heard that the Confederates were bringing up artillery to force him to surrender.

This situation forced Porter to call off his advance, and he turned back to try to reach Sherman's trailing infantry. For a time Porter feared that he might have to scuttle his boats and head overland through the swamps to the Mississippi. His fears were allayed when Sherman pushed his troops forward as fast as he could to relieve Porter on the 21st, just in time to drive off

the arriving Confederate infantry. But Porter was still not out of danger. He had to back his gunboats down Steele's Bayou stern first for over thirty miles, a trip that took three days to complete.

Sherman's bayou expeditions thus returned to its base in failure on 27 March, convincing Grant that the Fort Pemberton attack should also be called off. He ordered Quinby and Ross to return to the Mississippi as fast as they could. They received this order on 1 April, and withdrew from Fort Pemberton on the 5th.

Confederate snipers harass a Federal ironclad during Steele's Bayou expedition.

Grant's Generals

Grant's victory at Vicksburg was helped by the fact that he had a strong supporting cast of Generals. His alter ego, William T. Sherman, commander of the 15th corp, understood Grant's intentions perfectly and played a key role at every stage of the campaign. Grant in fact only had one weak and unreliable major commander — John A. McClernand, whom Grant fired in June as commander of the 13th Corps.

James B. McPherson, commander of the 17th Corps at Vicksburg, was almost as strong a leader as Sherman. He was born in Ohio in 1828 and graduated 1st in the West Point Class of 1853. He then entered the Engineer Corps, and served as Grant's Chief Engineer at Fort Donelson and Shiloh. In August 1862 he transferred to the infantry, and rose to the rank of Major General by October. He handled his corps very well throughout the Vicksburg campaign, and played an especially key role at Champion Hill.

McPherson showed such great promise that he was given command of the Army of the Tennessee when Sherman succeeded Grant as supreme General in the West. He fought well in the Atlanta campaign until he was killed in action on 22 July 1864. He and John F. Reynolds (killed at Gettysburg on 1 July 1863) were the two highest ranking Union Generals killed in action during the war.

E.O.C. Ord, McClernand's replacement as commander of the 13th Corps was also an excellent commander with a promising future. He was born in Maryland in 1818 and graduated from West Point in 1839. He began the Civil War as a Brigadier General in Virginia. Later he was promoted to Major General and was transferred to the West, where he was wounded at the battle of Corinth. His return to duty gave Grant the opportunity to can McClernand during the height of the siege or Vicksburg.

Ord went east with Grant in 1864 and received command of the 18th Corps. Later he became commander of the Army of the James. It was said of Ord that he rose to higher command than his abilities actually warranted because of his close friendship with

James B. McPherson (center) with his chief engineers.

Grant. He died in Havana, Cuba, in 1883.

Grant's most aggressive division commander was John A. Logan. Logan was born in Illinois in 1826, and had very limited military experience before the war. He instead was by occupation a lawyer and politician, a die hard member of the Democratic party. At the beginning of the war, his allegiance was suspect because of his harsh opinion of Negroes and his connections to the pro-Confederate sections of Southern Illinois. These suspicions were erased when he threw all his efforts into recruiting and even raised his own regiment. He won distinction at Belmont and Fort Donelson, and was promoted to Brigadier General through President Lincoln's policy of promoting popular Democrats (the most noted example of this policy was George B. McClellan).

Logan's skills made him a favorite of both Grant and Sherman. He rose to the rank of Major General in November 1862, and led a division of the 17th Corps in the Vicksburg Campaign. In 1864 he became commander of the 15th Corps, and even led the Army of the Tennessee for awhile after James McPherson was killed at Atlanta.

Logan campaigned for the Republicans in 1864, and after the war used the war issue to keep himself in political power. He served long stints in the U.S. Congress and Senate as a Radical Republican, and often raised the "bloody shirt" issue against peace Democrats and ex-Confederates. He was active in Veterans' groups and helped establish Memorial Day as a holiday. Logan died in Washington D.C. in 1886.

Grant had another strong political general in his command, Frank Blair Jr. Blair was born in Kentucky in 1821 and belonged to a very strong political family that helped keep Missouri in the Union in 1861. His father was a good friend of Andrew Jackson and was a key early backer and advisor of Abraham Lincoln's national political career; his brother, Montgomery Blair, was Lincoln's first Postmaster General.

John Alexander Logan.

Before the war, Blair was a lawyer, not a military man. When the war began he used his political influence to recruit seven Missouri regiments, and was appointed a Brigadier General. He led a division in the 15th Corps during the Vicksburg Campaign, and was promoted to command of the 15th Corps at Chattanooga. During the Atlanta campaign he transferred to the command of the 17th Corps, which he led until the close of the War.

After the war, Blair stayed in law and politics. He died in St. Louis in 1875.

E.O.C. Ord with his family.

That Devil Forrest

Nathan Bedford Forrest was perhaps the war's greatest cavalry commander. What he accomplished was purely by instinct, since he had no professional military training. He was born in Bedford, Tennessee, in 1821 to a poor blacksmith who died when Nathan was 16. Through his own efforts and ingenuity he rose to be a wealthy trader and plantation owner before the war.

When the war began, Forrest volunteered as a private. His talents were so great that he quickly rose to Brigadier General in July 1862, Major General in December 1863, and Lieutenant General just before the war ended. No other soldier is known to have made such a leap in the war, from private to Lieutenant General in just four years. Some of his mottoes became legendary, especially "Get there first with the most", and "war means fightin' and fightin' means killin'".

Forrest's wartime heroism began at Fort Donelson, where he refused to be taken prisoner when the post was surrendered unconditionally to General U.S. Grant in February 1862. Instead, he found an unguarded path and boldly led his whole regiment to safety.

At Shiloh in April, Forrest was so restless while being held in reserve that he led a mounted charge against the Union "Hornets Nest" line. He was lucky to live to tell of his charge. It was for his heroism here that he was promoted to Brigadier General.

It was as a raider that Forrest earned his greatest reputation. His first great raid was in July 1862 when he led 1400 men into central Tennessee. There he surprised and captured Brigadier General Thomas L. Crittenden and the 1000 man garrison of Murfreesboro on July 14. A week later he made a dash to the outskirts of Nashville, causing consternation and confusion in all the Union rear areas in Tennessee.

Forrest and his raiding ability had a great impact on the Vicksburg campaign when he destroyed Grant's supply lines in western Tennessee in December 1862 during Grant's first drive on Vicksburg. Forrest at the time was

One of the greatest cavalry commanders of the war, Nathan Bedford Forrest.

commanding a 2000 man cavalry brigade in Bragg's army of Tennessee. The raid began on 15 December and was first directed at Lexington, Tennessee. There he defeated a Union Cavalry force sent to intercept him. The next day he moved toward Jackson, Tennessee, and set about tearing up track of the Mobile and Ohio and Mississippi Central railroads. His rapid activity so awed Union General Jeremiah Sullivan that he stayed within his defenses at Jackson even though he had four times as many men as Forrest.

In the next few days Forrest continued to tear up railroad tracks on the Mobile and Ohio. He then invaded Kentucky and made it to within 10 miles of Columbus with no opposition. By now he realized that there were a great many Yankee cavalry units after him, so he headed to Huntington, north of Lexington, Tennessee. At Parker's crossroads he ran into two cavalry brigades led by General Sullivan on 31 December. In a confused engagement Forrest lost all his cannons but captured 300 Yankees. He then returned to his starting point on 1 January, having achieved a total success. Combined with Van Dorn's capture of Holly Spring, Forrest's railroad wrecking in Tennessee forced Grant to abandon his invasion of Mississippi and even contributed to Sherman's bad defeat at Chickasaw Bluffs at the end of December 1862.

Forrest missed the remainder of the Vicksburg campaign when he returned to service with Bragg's army in eastern Tennessee. While there he went to meet a raid led by Union Colonel Abel Streight, who had most of his men mounted on mules. Forrest captured Streight's entire command at Cedar Bluff, Alabama, on 3 May.

Forrest's next great escapade was at the Battle of Brice's Cross Roads, Mississippi, in June, 1864. At that time Sherman was operating against Atlanta, and was becoming nervous about the possibility of Forrest attacking his lengthening supply lines. For this reason he sent Brigadier General Samuel Sturgis with 8000 men to seek out and destroy Forrest's command at any cost. Forrest prepared a defensive position at Brice's Cross Roads and defeated Sturgis' cavalry (led by Brigadier General Benjamin Grierson) when it came up on the morning of 10 June. He then routed Sturgis' infantry as they rushed up, exhausted, to Grierson's aid. The battle, which is considered Forrest's masterpiece, cost him 500 casualties while he inflicted over 2200.

One of Forrest's earlier escapades was not as glorious as his victory at Brice's Cross Roads. In April 1864 he commanded the troops that captured Fort Pillow, Tennessee, and allegedly massacred a number of captured Negro troops. Forrest's role in the massacre has never been satisfactorily explained.

After the war, Forrest became wealthy again as a planter. He was one of the founders of the Ku Klux Klan, and may have been its first Grand Wizard. He died in Memphis in 1877.

CHAPTER VII

GRANT'S FINAL DRIVE

The failure of all four projects attempted since the end of January (the Desoto Canal, Lake Providence expedition, Yazoo Pass Project, and Steele's Bayou expedition) left Grant in a most awkward position. Though his troops had been encamped for nearly three months at Young's Point, almost in sight of Vicksburg, he was still no closer to capturing the Confederate fortress than he had been when he first moved against Holly Springs. Three options now lay before him. One was to assault Vicksburg at the Chickasaw Bluffs where Sherman had attacked in December; Grant dismissed this as too costly, especially in view of the increased size of the Vicksburg garrison (now at 30,000). A second option was to return to Memphis and attack either Holly Springs or Grenada; Grant dismissed this choice because he had already attempted it unsuccessfully the previous December. This left him with his third option: to move his entire command south of Vicksburg through the more open country to its southeast.

To carry out this project, Grant needed to clear an all-water route for his supply transports from his base at Milliken's Bend to a point near New Carthage, about 30 miles below Vicksburg. His plan was to gather as many supply transports as he could at New Carthage, and use them to carry his troops across the river to capture Grand Gulf. Once he possessed Grand Gulf, he would be free to operate at will in the rear of Vicksburg. Before he did this, though, he was urged by General Halleck to help Banks capture Port Hudson. Then Grant's and Banks' combined armies would be free to move jointly on Vicksburg.

Grant takes to the field.

Soldiers of McClernand's corps lay corduroy roads for Grant's march through Louisiana.

In preparation for the march south, Grant ordered Roundabout Bayou and other necessary waterways on the route to New Carthage cleared of obstructions. Water level on the appointed route was increased with waters diverted from the Mississippi via a short canal run from Duckport (opposite Young's Point) to Roundabout Bayou. Great care was taken to clear roads and build necessary bridges so most of the infantry could march south rather than have to rely on transports. This precaution proved to be a wise move, since the bayou system never was dredged out enough to be relied on for troop transport.

In order to distract Confederate attention from his move south, Grant sent Steele's division on an expedition to Greenville, some 150 miles above Vicksburg. Meanwhile McClernand's corps slowly moved south, to test the Roundabout Bayou passage. McClernand captured Richmond, Louisiana, on 31 March, and reached New Carthage on 6 April. He had his entire corps concentrated there by 20 April, poised to cross the Mississippi. Behind him, McPherson gathered his corps at Milliken's Bend, while Sherman formed up at Duckport and Young's Point.

Grant moved his headquarters to New Carthage on 23 April, only to find the town too low and waterlogged to be used as his jumping-off base. He also discovered by personal reconnaissance that the Confederate batteries at Grand Gulf were too strong to be attacked head on. For this reason, the ever resourceful Grant adjusted his plan and moved 15 miles downriver to a tiny town colorfully, named Hard Times. The actual river crossing, set for 29 April, would land at Bruinsburg, 10 miles south of Grand Gulf.

Pemberton, meanwhile, had been totally misled about Grant's intentions. His 50,000-man force was stretched over a 200-mile perimeter that ran from Fort Pemberton in the north to Port Hudson. W.W. Loring still held Fort Pemberton with 7,000 men, while Frank Gardner had 16,000 at Port Hudson. Another 5,000 were keeping an eye on Hurlbut's corps along the Memphis and Corinth Railroad. Pemberton's main force was his 22,000-man Vicksburg garrison, which he could use to reinforce Loring or other points as needed. A significant absence in his command was Van Dorn's 6,000-man cavalry force, which had been transferred to Braxton Bragg's army earlier in the year. Van Dorn's absence severely hampered Pemberton's movements in the coming campaign.

PILOT BREAD

Federals slog their way through Louisiana on their way to a crossing of the Mississippi.

Grierson's Raid

Benjamin Henry Grierson was one of the North's great cavalry commanders, and played a key role in the Vicksburg Campaign with his raid through Mississippi in April 1863. He was born in Pittsburgh in 1826, and was a businessman before the war. At the opening of the war, he enlisted as a private (just as did his fellow cavalry commander on the Confederate side, Nathan B. Forrest). By the end of 1861 he became a major in the 6th Illinois Cavalry, and was promoted to colonel in April 1862. His aggressive pursuit of Van Dorn's raiders after that Confederate's destruction of Grant's supply base at Holly Springs in December 1862 earned him a promotion to brigade command.

Grierson's moment of glory came in April 1863 when he was ordered by Grant to conduct a cavalry raid through eastern Mississippi and distract Pemberton's attention from Grant's pending flank movement south of Vicksburg. Grierson left La Grange, Tennessee, on 17 April at the head of 1700 troopers. As he headed south he ran into Confederate cavalry, so he sent Colonel Edward Hatch with one third of his force on a decoy raid towards the Mobile and Ohio railroad. When the Confederate cavalry followed Hatch, Grierson went on his way south. Hatch returned safely to La Grange.

Grierson reached Newton Station on 24 April, and set about wrecking the Southern Railroad. The Confederates were by now eager to catch him, but Pemberton lacked enough cavalry resources for the job. Grierson now opted to head west instead of north. He cut the New Orleans, Jackson and Great Northern Railroad and reached Union lines at Baton Rouge on 2 May. His raid had been a complete success by distracting Pemberton's attentions from Grant's movements, especially the river crossing to Bruinsburg on 29 April.

Grierson was rewarded for the success of the raid by a promotion to brigadier general. He finished the war in that capacity after having more than one encounter with that nemesis of all Union cavalry, Nathan B. Forrest.

Grierson stayed in the cavalry after the war as colonel of the 10th U.S. Calvary. He fought many campaigns against the Indians and rose to the rank of brigadier general in the Regular Army. He died in Michigan in 1911.

Pemberton was well aware of the natural strength of the river bluffs at Grand Gulf, which he had ordered to be occupied and fortified on 5 March because of Grant's progress on the DeSoto Point canal. At the end of April, the post was occupied by four batteries and a 2,500-man Missouri brigade led by Brigadier General J.S. Bowen. Bowen had sent three regiments across the river to oppose McClernand's advance on New Carthage, but they were not strong enough to do anything except report the stages of McClernand's advance.

Pemberton was frankly confused about Grant's intentions. His opponent's probing expeditions since January had thrown him off balance. For this reason he was not particularly concerned about McClernand's advance to New Carthage. In fact, at the time he was paying more attention to Steele's division operating north of Vicksburg on his more vulnerable flank near Fort Pemberton. He also thought Sherman might be preparing to attack Haynes' Bluff. Grierson's late April cavalry raid also posed a problem, particularly because Pemberton had little cavalry available to oppose him (see sidebar). One area that definitely was not a concern to the Confederate commander was Port Hudson. General Banks, who had been operating in the area after his advance from Baton Rouge, had wandered off into western Louisiana and was not at the moment posing any threat to Port Hudson.

Porter's flotilla passes by the Vicksburg batteries on its way to join Grant below the town.

Port Hudson—The First Assault

The siege of Port Hudson was conducted as a necessary adjunct to the more important siege of Vicksburg, about 130 miles to the north. The Confederate commander at Port Hudson, Major General Frank Gardner, had only about 7000 men and was totally outnumbered by Nathaniel P. Banks' Union force of over 20,000. Consequently, the Confederates had little choice but to endure the privations of the siege, which were more severe—and less well known—than those at Vicksburg.

Port Hudson had first been fortified in August of 1862, when General John C. Breckinridge ordered heavy batteries to be built to control the river after his unsuccessful attempt to wrest control of Baton Rouge from the Union forces. Port Hudson is located on the east side of the Mississippi about twenty-five miles north of Baton Rouge. Its military significance stems from the fact that there are 80-foot high bluffs near the town that dominate a sharp bend of the river. Here some 20 heavy siege cannons were placed to blast any Union ships attempting to come upstream against the river's current.

On its landward side Port Hudson was protected by over three miles of works. These ran in a broad arc from Ross's Landing, a mile south of Port Hudson, to the mouth of Thompson's Creek, one-half mile north of the town. The defenses were built by slave labor and consisted of a ditch about 15 feet deep in front of a parapet about 20 feet thick. The line was augmented by four small forts—one at the southern apex of the line at Ross's Landing, one at the southeast corner of the works, another along the main road to Baton Rouge, and the fourth near Thompson's Creek. These forts and nearby embrasures were equipped with 30 pieces of field artillery. The whole position was well served by an interior road net that aided communications. The landward defenses were strongest at their southern end at Ross's Landing. East of Ross's Landing, the lines ran through a broad plain and so were readily accessible to an attack. The northern part of the line was stronger since the terrain there was rougher and full of ravines.

Commander of the Confederate garrison at Port Hudson, Franklin Gardner.

Most of the Port Hudson defenses were constructed under the direction of Brigadier General William Beall, who took command of the post on 25 September 1862. Beall stayed on as a brigade commander when Major General Frank Gardner became commander at Port Hudson on 28 December. In March 1863 the strength of his garrison grew from 12,000 to a peak of about 20,000. This number was greatly reduced in late April when Gardner was ordered to send two brigades (Gregg's and Maxey's) to Jackson to help block Grant's final drive on Vicksburg. This left Gardner with around 7000 men when Banks began the siege. The troops were loosely organized into three brigades, commanded by Brigadier General William Beall, and Colonels W.R. Miles and I.G.W. Steedman.

Banks had been maneuvering against Vicksburg for several months, but did not actually begin the siege until 25 May. He might not have even begun the siege then, had he not received specific instructions from Grant to do so. Grant had just begun the siege of Vicksburg on 22 May, and he was anxious to prevent Gardner's command from leaving Port Hudson to join Pemberton at Vicksburg or Confederate forces elsewhere. In fact, Pemberton himself was afraid of Gardner's command being trapped at Port Hudson, and on 19 May sent him orders to evacuate the post. Unfortunately, Gardner did not receive the orders until 24 May, when Banks was so near the town that the Confederates

could not withdraw safely.

Banks had been campaigning in the Red River Valley on the western side of the Mississippi when he received Grant's order to invest Port Hudson. His command reached the Mississippi on 23 May. After crossing, he began approaching the town from the east on 24 May, just in time to prevent Gardner's command from escaping, as already mentioned. Banks then spent all of 25 May arranging his forces opposite the Confederate works. Brigadier General T.W. Sherman's division was placed on the left, Major General Christopher C. Augur's division was in the center, and Brigadier General Cuvier Grover's division with Brigadier General Godfrey Weitzel's brigade of Auger's division were assigned the right of the line.

Now that his troops were in position, Banks decided to attempt to carry the Confederate works by direct assault on the morning of 27 May. In preparation for the assault, the Union artillery opened fire a 0545. The infantry was supposed to attack in unison all along the line, but coordination proved difficult to achieve—a problem Civil War commanders on both sides met in numerous battles.

As things developed, Weitzel's brigade on the right was the first to advance on the enemy. Weitzel began moving about 0600, and immediately ran into all kinds of difficulty. Firstly, the ground over which he was to advance was so full of ravines and underbrush that the soldiers had difficulty keeping in line, or even seeing where they were going. This same heavy terrain made it hard for the selected volunteers to carry the bundles of sticks (fascines) that were thought to be necessary to fill in the moat in front of the Confederate defenses. The bundles were simply too long, heavy and cumbersome to be dragged through the brush, and most had to be abandoned.

Weitzel's third problem was totally unanticipated. The Confederate commander on the left, Colonel I.G.W. Steedman, had decided he had too few men (only 1600) to hold his position against an assault, since his men could be posted no closer than one every five feet. In addition, most of his men were armed with smoothbore muskets that fired buckshot, which was deadly but had limited range. Steedman decided to meet the Yankee advance in front of his lines, and posted 500 men about half a mile out. This detachment hid behind fallen trees until the Yankee line came into range. Their unexpected volley shattered Weitzel's first line in what one soldier called "a huge bushwhack."

Weitzel soon recovered his composure, and his superior forces began driving Steedman's detachment back to the main Confederate line on Commissary Hill. Weitzel formed his men and directed an advance on a wide front. The Confederate fire was devastating, and mowed down the bravest Yankees who advanced the hardest. Especially hard pressed were those Yankees who advanced into an apparent gap in the Confederate line between Commissary Hill and a strong point to the east called Fort Desperate. This gap, called the Bull Pen, turned into a slaughterhouse for the attackers.

As Weitzel's losses mounted, the cohesion of his troops began to melt. Matters were not helped any by the loss of the colonels of the 1st Louisiana, 38th Massachusetts and 8th New Hampshire. To make matters worse, the dry brush caught fire in some

Confederate works at Port Hudson, Mississippi.

places, burning helpless wounded soldiers to death. The artillerymen of the 1st Maine Battery faced quite a different problem. As they moved into position to support the advancing infantry, the cannoneers began to wonder why the Confederates had nailed white crosses to the trees. A barrage of accurate and deadly enemy fire immediately showed them that the crosses were not religious in purpose, but were premeasured range finders set up by Confederate artillerists.

Weitzel now realized that the Confederate defense was too determined to carry. He had no choice but to begin to call his attackers back to positions of greater safety.

Meanwhile, Grover's division on Weitzel's left also moved into action. Grover, too, met heavy enemy fire, especially from Fort Desperate. This fire stalled his advance some 200 yards from the enemy works. An impasse now developed on the Union right as Grover held up waiting for Weitzel to advance again, and Weitzel held up his bloodied regiments waiting for support from Grover.

While his attack stalled on his front, Weitzel tried to gain an advantage on the Confederates by sending two regiments under Brigadier General William Dwight to attack the far Confederate left. Chosen for the task were two untested regiments of Black troops (the 1st and 3rd Louisiana), who were given an impossible task. The Confederate line they attacked was well entrenched on a high bluff, and was extremely well supported by artillery.

Godfrey Weitzel.

William Dwight.

Dwight's attackers hardly had a chance, even though they faced only about 300 Confederate defenders from the 39th Mississippi. Concentrated Confederate fire blasted away and drove the Blacks to seek any shelter at hand; one Confederate defender later wrote that "we moad [mowed] them down." The few attackers who bravely pushed on soon found themselves facing a stream 40 feet wide and 6 to 8 feet deep. A squad of 40 men attempted to cross, but only 6 returned.

Thus Dwight's attack met a bloody repulse. Dwight himself was furious, and ordered the assault renewed. His officers cringed at the order, and refused to obey when they realized that their commander was drunk. They understood that no amount of gallantry could carry the Confederate bluffs. Their Black troops had lost over 150 men in their charge. The Confederate defenders had not lost a man.

Augur's brigade experienced a different form of difficulty attacking the Confederate center. It seems that the Confederates had felled all the trees for more than a mile in front of this portion of their line; the uncut tree branches made such a tangle that troops could not advance in good order. While the troops floundered through the felled trees, they were under the open fire of the Confederate batteries. These difficulties slowed Augur's advance considerably. He also did not put all his energy into the assault because he was waiting in vain for support from Sherman's division on his left.

Banks was disappointed at Sherman's failure to move, and late in the morning rode personally to the left to order him forward. When Sherman protested that any direct assault

would be suicidal, Banks exploded in anger and fired him on the spot, to be replaced by the army's chief of staff, Brigadier General George Andrews.

It took awhile for a messenger to find Andrews and guide him to Sherman's lines. When Andrews arrived, he found Sherman mounted up and ready to lead the ordered charge. He also appeared to be drunk. Andrews decided to hang back and watch Sherman lead the charge. It was a wise move by Andrews. A Confederate soldier saw Sherman advancing in front of his men: "The enemy advanced in beautiful formation, led by a general officer and staff, who rode together in advance of the colors." Sherman was a sitting duck in such an exposed position. Soon two of his staff members were shot, and his own horse went down. The brash general advanced on foot, only to be felled by grapeshot. He later lost his leg to an amputation, and was fortunate not to lose his life.

The ground over which Sherman attacked was ironically named Slaughter's Field after a local farmer. The field appeared open enough at first glance, but its gullies and stumps soon broke up the advancing lines. Then came the blazing enemy fire. This was so fierce that no Yankees got close to the ditch in front of the Confederate works. First Dow's brigade attacked and was repulsed. Then Nickerson's brigade advanced, including the Zouaves of the 165th New York with their red fezzes and baggy red Turkish pantaloons.

Soldiers of the 2nd Louisiana during their brave but fruitless rush against the Confederate position at Port Hudson held by the 39th Mississippi.

Amazingly, the Zouaves charged without stopping to fire. They just kept shouting "Huzzah Huzzah Huzzah" and kept advancing, taking casualties at every step. First their colonel went down, then their major. Finally they stopped to shoot before the intense enemy fire caused them to break and melt away.

When the 165th New York infantry, Duryea's Zouaves, were repulsed at Slaughter's Field at Port Hudson on 27 May, three of the strangely dressed Zouaves were seen sitting in a circle having a conversation. The Confederate defenders watched them with amazement, so oblivious to the slaughter around them. One Confederate sniper, though, was still intent on his work. He fired and felled one of the three Zouaves. This drove the other two to flee. The sniper's action was not applauded by his fellows.

At the same time, the New York state flag of the Zouave regiment could be seen lying on the field where its guard had fallen, some 70 yards from the Confederate line. One 15-year-old Louisiana infantryman named Will Clark decided to rush out and grab the flag, but was stopped by his commander who scolded, "You'll be killed out there." While they were conversing, another soldier named Matt Howley darted out and retrieved the flag. Clark angrily shouted at his commander, "Look, Matt got the flag, and he didn't get killed either."

While Sherman's men were being slaughtered in Slaughter's Field, Banks ordered Augur's division to assault the Confederate center. Augur did not advance until 1400, because of an hour's delay in locating the fascines needed to fill in the Confederate moat. It would be Augur's misfortune to strike Beall's brigade, the strongest Confederate command at Port Hudson. Their fire was so intense that "human endurance was not equal to the task" of resisting it. Yankees fell by the score, and most dove for cover, unable to advance or retreat until dark. Only a few came even close to the Confederate works. Most fell casualty. One who did not was Henry C. Johns of the 49th Massachusetts. He fixed his bayonet and charged the Confederate line with a score of fellows, and was one of the few to return unscathed. For this act he received the Congressional Medal of Honor.

Throughout the day Banks wasted his men in a series of disjointed assaults. The final attack of the day came on the right, where Grover's reserve of four regiments (1300 men) was sent forward about 1230. It took them over an hour to advance through the heavy terrain and reach the enemy position. They then assaulted one of the Confederates' strongest positions —Fort Desperate—head on.

Grover's attack met no more success than any other Union attack that bloody day. Soon his regiments were pinned down, unable to advance or retreat. Then a miracle occurred. At

about 1730 some Yankees raised white flags, and the Confederate defenders accepted their offer for a truce. Soon troops of both sides who had just been shooting at each other were now conversing amiably. Under protection of the truce, the Yankees who had been pinned down simply got up and walked away. Needless to say, the Confederate officers were furious at the situation. Even so, the white flags did not come down until 1900. The firing then picked up as if there had been no truce.

As the fighting finally ceased for the day, both sides lay back to count their casualties. Banks officially reported about 2000 casualties: 293 killed, 1545 wounded and 157 missing. His actual losses were probably closer to 3000, almost 25 percent of his engaged force. Confederate losses were only about 350; of these 156 had occurred in two regiments (15th Arkansas and 1st Alabama) who held Fort Desperate. It had indeed been a disastrous day for the Yankees.

In another of Bank's fatal assaults against Port Hudson, members of Augurs division struggle to cross acres of felled trees to reach Confederate fortifications. This attack also met a bloody repulse.

Grant's movements were also confusing to General A.S. Johnston, Confederate overall commander in the western theater since the previous December. At his headquarters at Jackson, Mississippi, Johnston felt Grant would not be attempting anything significant for while. In fact, his intelligence sources led him to believe that Banks was invading the Red River district again and Grant was going to return to Memphis, possibly to reinforce Rosecrans in eastern Tennessee. For this reason he transferred a brigade of 4,000 men from Port Hudson to Vicksburg and was making preparations to transfer other troops from Pemberton's army to Chattanooga.

Grant's final drive on Vicksburg commenced at 0700 on 29 April 1862, when Porter's squadron of seven gunboats carrying 81 guns left Hard Times to bombard the Confederate batteries at Grand Gulf and clear the way for the infantry transports to cross. The cannonade opened at 0800 and continued for five hours, silencing the Grand Gulf batteries but not destroying them. In the process, several of Porter's boats were badly hurt from the plunging enemy fire.

Because the Grand Gulf batteries were still effective, Grant did not send his infantry transports across the river until after dark. Porter kept up a covering fire, and the transports all made it safely across to Bruinsburg. By noon of 30 April, McClernand had all four of his divisions across the river. His landing had been totally unopposed, thanks largely to the confusion Grierson's raid had caused for the Confederates. The movement was also aided by a demonstration Sherman staged at Haynes' Bluff on 30 April and 1 May. Sherman's maneuver was so successful that it temporarily froze all of Pemberton's command in the Vicksburg defenses. Pemberton was even so fooled that he recalled 3,000 men that had been sent on their way to reinforce the garrison at Grand Gulf.

A Federal transport or "cotton-clad" safely passes the Vicksburg batteries protected by a barge of cotton secured to its hull.

Once McClernand's men landed, it was imperative for them to hurry forward three miles to seize the bluffs above Bruinsburg. Otherwise the Confederate reinforcements would occupy the position in strength, and Grant would have to fight his way through. However, McClernand felt he could not send his men forward because they had no rations. It seems that someone had forgotten to issue an order for the

John S. Bowen.

men to carry the usual three days' supply of food they carried at the start of every campaign. Since McClernand did not know how long his men would be fighting once they started marching out of Bruinsburg, he held the whole column back for four hours while rations were issued.

McClernand's delay was the kind of mistake that often could lead to the loss of a battle. Fortunately for him, there were no Confederate troops on the nearby bluffs to stop his advance when his lead elements arrived there at sunset. McClernand pushed on towards Port Gibson, some ten miles distant. Grant was anxious to seize that point in order to outflank the Confederate works at Grand Gulf and because it controlled the roads to the interior. McClernand's leading troops ran into Confederate troops just after midnight about four miles out of Port Gibson. Rather than risk an engagement with unknown troops on unfamiliar ground, McClernand ordered his troops to lay on their arms until dawn.

The troops McClernand ran into outside of

Federal gunboats bombard the Confederate batteries at Grand Gulf to allow Grant's troops to cross over to the east bank of the Mississippi.

Port Gibson were part of Green's brigade, which Bowen had sent there from Grand Gulf on the afternoon of 30 April. Bowen had been alarmed by Porter's bombardment on 29 April and the fleet of transports he was heading downriver. His reports convinced Pemberton that the Yankees were making a major maneuver in that sector, so he began shifting troops to meet the threat. Pemberton sent Tracy's and Baldwin's brigades, about 5,000 men, from Vicksburg to Grand Gulf on the 29th. It was their arrival that enabled Bowen to send Green to Port Gibson. On the 30th, Pemberton also began gathering reserves at Jackson and Edwards' Station, while he himself transferred his headquarters from Jackson to Vicksburg.

While McClernand's men rested early in the morning of 1 May, Bowen sent Tracy's brigade to support Green at this main line three miles west of Port Gibson. McClernand began his attack at 0530, and had three divisions in action by 0700. The Confederates held on as best they could, but eventually had to begin to retire because they were so badly outnumbered. They fell back about a mile and found a new line formed by two fresh brigades under General Bowen, who had arrived at 0900 from Grand Gulf.

Grant's Yankees skirmish with Confederates during his campaign against Vicksburg in late spring of 1863.

Bowen's four brigades of 8,000 men now held off most of McClernand's corps for the whole afternoon. The battle was not determined until after 1700, when Grant threw into action the advance units of McPherson's corps, which had just crossed the river. McPherson broke Bowen's right flank, and the Confederates withdrew from the field towards sunset. The daylong battle had cost them 787 casualties while they inflicted 849. The Confederate defenders had indeed fought well, but were unable to hold their lines against 20,000 Yankees.

As the battle of Port Gibson raged, Pemberton sent more reinforcements to Grand Gulf and ordered Loring's division to move from Grenada towards Port Gibson. The Confederate commander was faced with a great dilemma: how to deal with Grant's incursion and still hold on to his far flung posts at Fort Pemberton, Vicks-

burg, Port Hudson, Jackson, and points in- between. In the coming campaign, Pemberton would refuse to strip Vicksburg's defenses completely for fear that Grant would make a dash at the city. As a result, he did not have enough troops to defeat Grant in the field.

On 2 May, the day after the battle of Port Gibson, Union troops entered the town and set about rebuilding the bridge over the south fork of the Bayou Pierre that had been destroyed by Bowen during his retreat. The bridge was finished at 1600, and Grant's men marched on 8 miles to the Bayou Pierre, just in time to put out a fire on the bridge there.

Grant's rapid advance convinced Pemberton of the necessity to abandon Grand Gulf and concentrate his forces on the hills north of the Big Black River. For this reason he destroyed his batteries and blew up his magazines at Grand Gulf on 2 May; Porter's gunboats took possession of the mined fortress the next day. Bowen withdrew his somewhat battered division to Hankinson's Ferry, where he was joined by four brigades of Stevenson's division from Vicksburg. This combined force of 17,000 then withdrew behind the Big Black River to await Grant's next move.

An impasse developed for several days as Pemberton solidified his position behind the Big Black and Grant waited for Sherman's troops to arrive. Grant was also burning up the telegraph wires trying to get into contact with General Banks. He had promised Halleck he would send

Since Grant cut his lines of communications and supplies during his march against Jackson and Vicksburg, his soldiers were forced to forage throughout the Mississippi countryside.

"Napoleon" P. Banks

Major General Nathaniel P. Banks was one of the numerous politician-generals that plagued both sides during the Civil War. He was born in 1816 in Waltham, Massachusetts, and had no military experience before the war. His principal pre-war occupation was politics. He was originally a member of the Democratic Party, and as such served in the Massachusetts legislature (1849-1852). In 1853 he was elected to the National Congress as a Democrat, but soon switched allegiance to the Republican Party. Banks was a powerful member of Congress until 1857, when he resigned to become governor of Massachusetts (1858-1861). His final pre-war job was a brief but lucrative stint as vice-president of the Illinois Central Rail Road (Union General George B. McClellan was also a vice-president of this same railroad).

When the war began, Banks received an appointment as major general of U.S. Volunteers solely because he was a good Republican with powerful political connections. His first assignment was an administrative one in Annapolis, Maryland. He was there given field command of the Department of the Shenandoah (later XII Corps, Army of the Potomac). In this role he was the principal opponent to Stonewall Jackson in the 1862 Shenandoah Valley Campaign. His troops beat Jackson at Kernstown on 23 March 1862, one of the few battles Jackson lost in the war; however, Banks was not present on the field and the battle was directed by his subordinates. Banks was then totally outgeneraled by Jackson, who marched at will up and down the Valley. Jackson's most notable victories over Banks were at Winchester on May 25 and Port Republic on 9 June. Jackson captured so many supplies from Banks that he took to calling his opponent "Commissary" Banks.

Banks was retained in high command despite his thrashing at Jackson's hands. Now commanding the II Corps of the Army of Virginia, he achieved initial success against Jackson at Cedar Mountain on 9 August 1862. By then Lincoln realized that Banks had more administrative ability than skills at field generalship. Consequently Banks was reassigned during the pre-Antietam army reorganization. His new command was the high profile but relatively safe Department of Washington, D.C.

Banks, however, still yearned for the glory of field command. In November 1862, after only a month in command at Washington, he got himself appointed as successor of General Ben "Beast" Butler as commander of the Department of the Gulf, headquartered at New Orleans. His instructions were to cooperate with General Grant in clearing the Mississippi; when this was accomplished, he was to proceed west to occupy the Red River basin,

After taking command in New Orleans on 16 December 1862, Banks immediately occupied Baton Rouge. Then, instead of advancing against the Confederate garrison at Port Hudson, only twenty-five miles upstream, he turned his attention to Galveston, Texas, some 200 miles to the west! This attack fizzled when the invaders were captured by the Confederate defenders on 1 January 1863.

Banks now turned his full attention back to his proper assignment, the clearing of the Mississippi. His primary goal now was to capture Port Hudson. Since he heard that Port Hudson was garrisoned by over 15,000 Confederates, a force the size of his own field command, Banks was reluctant to attack straight on. Instead, he decided first to capture the west bank of the Mississippi, opposite Port Hudson, an area that furnished Port Hudson with most of its supplies. This expedition, which lasted from 9 April to 7 May, was largely inconclusive. Its major achievement was to take Banks away from the Mississippi, so preventing him from cooperating with Grant during the latter's drive on Vicksburg.

Once Grant began besieging Vicksburg, Banks crossed to the east bank of the Mississippi to attack Port Hudson. The siege saw several unsuccessful assaults and was not conducted unusually well by Banks, who had at least a 2-1 strength advantage over the defenders. Despite extreme hunger, the Confederates held on until they heard Vicksburg had surrendered and realized further resistance was hopeless. Port Hudson surrendered on 9 July and earned Banks the official thanks of

Congress "for the skill, courage, and endurance which compelled the surrender of Port Hudson and thus removed the last obstruction to the free navigation of the Mississippi River."

It was an invigorated Banks who led a new invasion of the Red River basin in the spring of 1864. His goal was to reach Texas, but he soon found himself totally outgeneraled by Lieutenant General Dick Taylor, who had been one of Jackson's generals in the 1862 Shenandoah Valley Campaign. The Red River Campaign ended a total failure in May. Banks was fired from army command; his poor performance was censured by Congress and investigated by the Joint Committee on the Conduct of the War.

Banks was shelved until the end of the war — he was a general without a command until he resigned on 24 August 1865. He had shown himself to be a competent military administrator, but he simply lacked enough military sense or background to do well in the field. His one great success was almost accidental; just about any Union commander with his wits about him could have captured Port Hudson, which was always a sideshow to the more important siege at Vicksburg. What is most notable about Banks is the fact that he managed to hold command at such high rank for three whole years in spite of his inexperience. His nickname "Napoleon" P. Banks came from his at times imperious nature.

Following the War, Banks returned to his first love, politics. He served as U.S. congressman from Massachusetts from 1865-1873, 1875-1879 and 1889-1891, and held various other political posts when not in Congress. His total congressional career, before and after the war, covered almost 20 years. He had to retire from Congress in 1891 because of "increasing mental disorder," and died on 1 September 1894, in his home at Waltham, Massachusetts.

Nathaniel Banks (center with arms crossed) with his staff.

a corps to help Banks reduce Port Hudson, but Banks was not immediately to be found. Eventually he was located in backwoods Louisiana, where he had been chasing Breckinridge's command. From there Banks reported he could not reach the Mississippi for a couple weeks.

Grant now had to make the best of the altered situation. He sent orders to Banks to move against Port Hudson as soon as he could; Banks would begin a siege there on 27 May (see sidebars). Grant then made the bold decision to move against Vicksburg by himself. He knew that it might be months before Banks took Port Hudson, and he wanted to exploit his present advantage while Pemberton was off balance and before the enemy was reinforced. His new plan was to avoid Pemberton's strong line on the Big Black River and head north toward Edwards' Station. He would then be able to cut Vicksburg's main supply route to Jackson, and also deal with the force that Johnston was gathering in the Mississippi capital. Such a move would also stretch Pemberton's line along the Big Black until it could be easily broken.

The biggest drawback in Grant's strategy was the fact that he would have to abandon his proposed base at Grand Gulf and live off the land. He had enough wagons with him (two per regiment) only for his ammunition, not for food or other supplies. Grant boldly made his decision to proceed anyway. He ordered his men to prepare five days' rations before setting out. They would have to forage for food from the countryside. His wagons would carry only ammunition. The men could fight without food, but they could not fight without bullets.

Grant began this new phase of the campaign on 11 May from his camp at Rocky Springs. He advanced on a broad front with Sherman in the center, McClernand on the left, closer to the Big Black River, and McPherson on the right, closer to Jackson. The force did not meet any real Confederate resistance until McPherson's advance under Major General John A. Logan ran into Brigadier General John Gregg's 3,000-man brigade at Fourteen Mile Creek, two miles south of Raymond, at about 1100 on 12 May. Gregg was badly outnumbered and put up a very stiff fight until he was forced from the field at mid-afternoon. Union losses at the battle of Raymond ran to 432, while Gregg lost 505.

As Grant moved north, Pemberton shifted most of his available field command (Loring's, Bowen's and Stevenson's divisions) to Edwards' Station. Meanwhile J.E. Johnston was ordered by Richmond to proceed to Jackson and take charge of events in Mississippi. Johnston arrived on 13 May and by the next day gathered a force of 12,000 consisting of four brigades: Gist's brigade, which had just arrived from South Carolina; Maxey's brigade from Port Hudson; and Gregg's and Walker's brigades, which had fought at Raymond.

Grant now decided to deal with Johnston's command before turning on Pemberton; he did not want Johnston operating in his rear while he advanced on Vicksburg. On the 13th he sent McPherson's corps to Jackson, supported by Sherman. The two corps reached Jackson at 1000 on the 14th in a pouring rain storm. In view of the odds against him, Johnston directed his brigadiers to fight only a delaying action while he withdrew all the supplies and government property he could. Thus the "Battle of Jackson" was not a very long affair. Sherman attacked Gregg's brigade on the south side of town, and easily took the Confederate lines by 1300. McPherson met more opposition west of

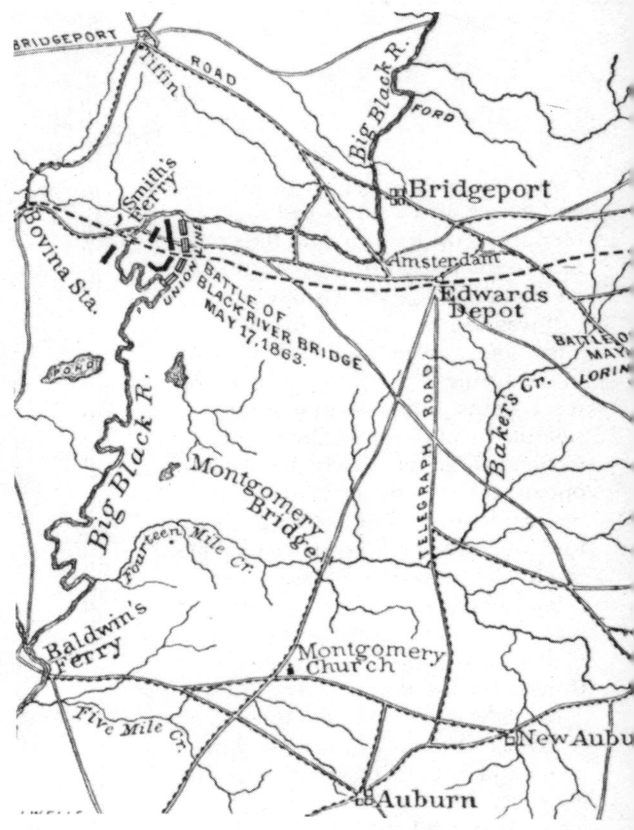

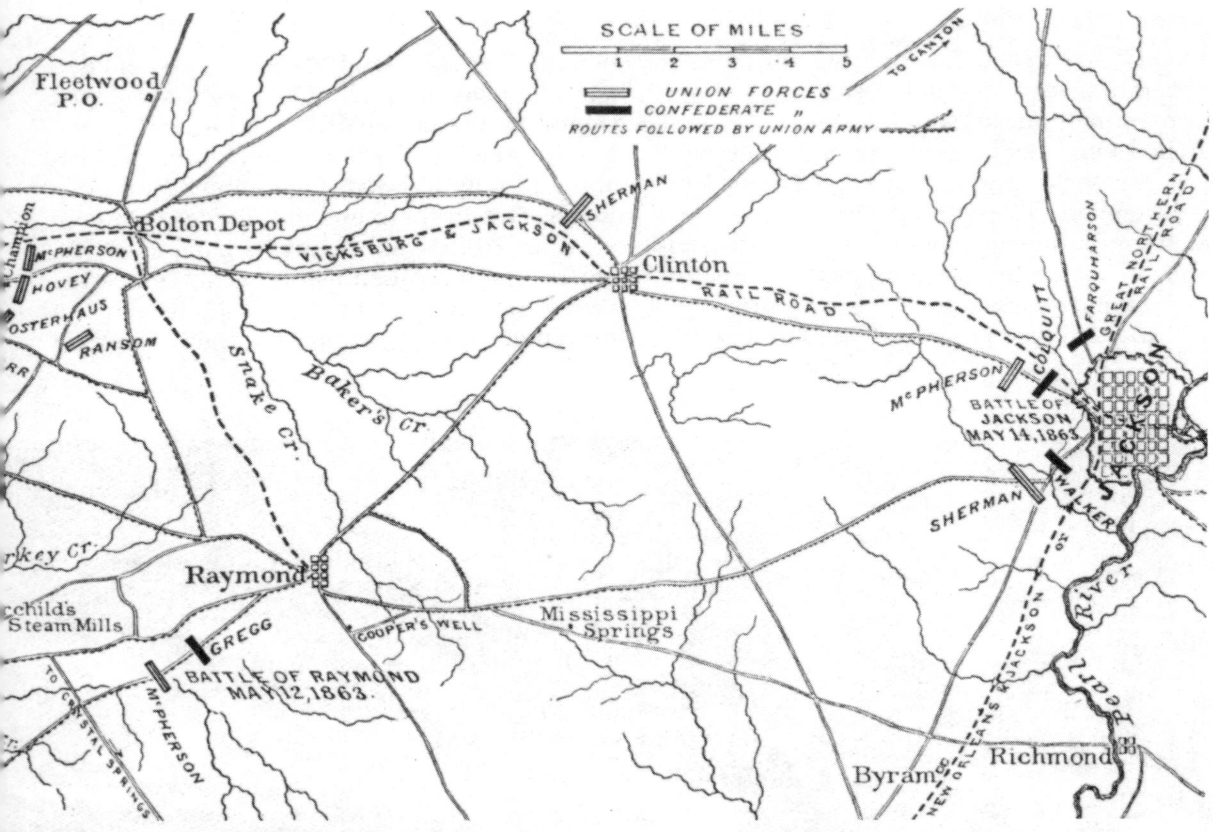

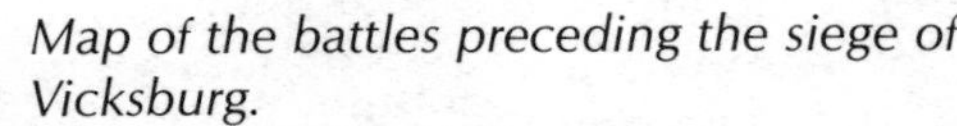
Map of the battles preceding the siege of Vicksburg.

town, when Walker's brigade put up a sharp fight before withdrawing. Thus by 1600 Grant had possession of Jackson, along with 17 cannons and over 800 prisoners. He could now turn his full attention to Pemberton's reduced command.

Pemberton now found himself faced with a further dilemma. Johnston gave him orders on 4 May to come out and strike Grant as soon as possible. Pemberton had other orders from President Davis to hold Vicksburg "at all costs." Since he was reluctant to uncover Vicksburg by joining Johnston, he called a council of his generals to discuss the situation. No one favored moving east, while a few suggested he should move to cut Grant's communication lines with the Mississippi. Pemberton vacillated for a day about what to do, and then had his choice thrust upon him: he found his lines at Champion's Hill suddenly under heavy attack on the morning of 16 May.

Before turning his attention to Vicksburg, Grant takes care of Joseph E. Johnston's command, engaging the Confederate force before Jackson, Mississippi.

Grant had wasted no time moving against Pemberton after he occupied Jackson. Leaving Sherman behind to watch Johnston, Grant marched with McPherson's corps directly west along the Vicksburg and Jackson Railroad toward Pemberton's position. McClernand, who had been skirmishing with Pemberton's command all during the drive on Jackson, was ordered to move towards the enemy from the southeast. Altogether Grant had almost 30,000 men ready to fight, facing about 22,000 in Pemberton's command. The odds were somewhat evened by the fact that Pemberton was on the defensive and held a moderately strong position atop a heavily wooded ridge fronted by a deep ravine. The northern end of the ridge culminated in an 80-foot hill, named Champion's Hill after a local plantation owner. Here Pemberton posted Stevenson's division, with Bowen's in the center and Loring's on the right, guarding

the road to Raymond.

The Battle of Champion's Hill began about 1030 on 16 May when Brigadier General Hovey's division of Sherman's corps began to assault Stevenson's line on the hill. The first attack, made with fixed bayonets by McGinnis' brigade, carried the Confederate line and captured a battery. Soon another battery fell. When Logan's Union division entered the battle on Hovey's right, Stevenson had no choice but to withdraw his whole line half a mile.

There was now a lull in the battle as McPherson consolidated his gains and waited for support on his left from McClernand, who was slow moving up. This delay enabled Pemberton to gain the upper hand in the battle. About 1300 he shifted Bowen's division to Stevenson's support. Then at 1430 he launched a savage counterattack that gained back all the losses of the morning and threatened to drive McPherson's two divisions from the field.

After seizing the capital of Mississippi, Sherman's troops set fire to Confederate warehouses and supplies.

Federal batteries pound Confederate positions.

J.E. Johnston, Military Enigma

Joseph Eggleston Johnston, overall Confederate commander in the West at the time of Vicksburg was one of the South's most distinguished generals in the war, even though he seldom won (or even fought) any major battles. Had his strategy in 1863 been followed, the siege of Vicksburg would probably never have happened and Pemberton's army of 20,000 would not have been captured. The reasons why Johnston's strategy was not followed stemmed largely from deficiencies in the Confederate command structure, difficulties that were very much the cause of Confederate defeat in the West, and from weaknesses in Johnston's personal character.

General Johnston was born in Farmville, Virginia, on 3 February 1807. He attended West Point as a classmate of Robert E. Lee, and graduated 13th in the class of 1829 (Lee ranked 2nd). His subsequent career as a lieutenant in the 4th Artillery led him to service in the Black Hawk War, the Seminole War, and other frontier campaigns. In 1837 he resigned from the army to become a civil engineer. This diversion from the military, however, did not last long. While working in Florida, he won attention for skillfully defending his survey party when it was attacked by Indians. This notice brought him an appointment as a 1st Lieutenant in the U.S. Topographical Engineers with the brevet (honorary) rank of captain.

Johnston served with distinction as a junior officer in the Mexican War. He was a member of General Winfield Scott's staff during the principal drive on Mexico City, and was in the thick of the fighting so often that he was wounded five times (and promoted three). His most heroic deed was to lead the storming column in the attack on Chapultepec, the principal fortress guarding Mexico City.

Johnston's military career continued to rise after the Mexican War. He served first as Chief of Topographical Engineers in Texas, and in 1855 was promoted to lieutenant colonel of the 1st U.S. Calvary. Efficient service in Kansas and the 1857 Utah expedition against the Mormons brought yet another promotion of the eve of the Civil War—he was named brigadier general

in charge of the U.S. Quartermaster Department on 28 June 1860.

Johnston resigned from the U.S. Army five days after Virginia seceded from the Union on April 17, 1861. His prewar service and reputation brought him immediate appointment as a major general of Virginia troops (Brigadier General CSA). His first assignment was the important post at Harper's Ferry. In July he skillfully slipped away from the opposing Union army, and joined General P.G.T. Beauregard's army at Manassas in time to defeat the Union forces at the battle of First Bull Run. As senior Confederate general at Bull Run, Johnston deserved more credit for the victory than he earned; Beauregard's more flamboyant nature stole some of his thunder.

Johnston's fine performance at Bull Run led to his promotion on 31 August to the rank of full General in the Confederate Army. This promotion, though, brought Johnston as much dissatisfaction as it did pleasure. It seems that Johnston expected to be ranked first among the Confederacy's full generals due to the fact that he had been senior brigadier general among the U.S. officers that sided with the South. Instead of being first, Johnston found himself ranked fourth, behind Samuel Cooper (the South's chief administrative officer who spent the whole war behind a desk in Richmond), Albert Sidney Johnston (no relation to J.E.; he was killed at Shiloh in April 1862), and Robert E. Lee.

Whether rightly or wrongly, Johnston blamed Confederate President Jefferson Davis for his lowered ranking on the list of full generals. Johnston's hard feelings on the issue provoked similar feelings from Davis. The two had never known each other well personally, and from then forward could deal with each other only coldly on the professional level. This animosity between the country's president and one of its top Generals did not bode well for the Confederacy, and caused severe repercussions during the 1863 Vicksburg Campaign.

For the moment, Johnston still stood in high graces. He was assigned the important Department of Virginia; his rival, Beauregard, was sent to the deep South. A.S. Johnston was sent west, and Lee was retained as Davis' personal military advisor.

Johnston's defensive and organizational talents served him well in his first major campaign, opposing McClellan's Army of the Potomac during 1862's Peninsula Campaign. When McClellan landed at Norfolk for an attack on Richmond from the east, Johnston urged the evacuation of all forward positions in order to defend a line closer to the capital. In this he was opposed by Davis, who ordered him to hold out in lines prepared on the old Revolutionary War battlefield at Yorktown. Here Davis' strategy proved best in the outcome. Johnston's delaying actions stalled McClellan long enough for the Confederates to eventually gather enough troops at Richmond to defeat the Yankee attack.

Johnston, however, was not destined to see the successful conclusion of the campaign. As McClellan was closing in on Richmond, Johnston ordered an attack at Seven Pines on 31 May. When the battle did not proceed as planned, he went forward to direct it personally. Just as darkness was bringing an end to the fighting, the General was wounded by a shell fragment. The wound took Johnston out of the war for almost six months. Command of his army was passed to Robert E. Lee, who led it to glory as commander of the Army of Northern Virginia for the remaining three years of the war.

When Johnston recovered from his wound in November, he was placed in command of the Department of the West, which was in strategic shambles due to the successes of Union General U.S. Grant. A.S. Johnston, Joseph Johnston's predecessor as head Confederate general in the West, had lost control of Tennessee before losing his life in a desperate battle at Shiloh. When Beauregard proved ineffective at commanding A.S. Johnston's army and Braxton Bragg led an ill-advised and ill-conducted invasion of Kentucky in late summer, J.E. Johnston was called on to bring stability to the theater.

Johnston was faced with a difficult problem of defending too much territory with too few troops and too few good generals. To accomplish his task he had two principal field armies, Pemberton's at Vicksburg (facing Grant) and Bragg's in central Tennessee (facing Rosecrans). Johnston also faced a potential threat of Union troops moving north from New Orleans.

Johnston found his efforts thwarted at almost every step by orders and interference from Richmond. The most significant disagreement over strategy came during the Vicksburg campaign. Johnston wanted to use Pemberton's army as a nucleus to form a field army big enough to meet Grant in the field. Davis, on the other hand, sent Pemberton orders to hold Vicksburg at all costs. Pemberton, faced with conflicting orders, chose to stay in Vicksburg. As a result, he was besieged and his army lost. Johnston did his best to gather a relieving army at Jackson, but it formed too late to be of help to Pemberton. Johnston was not able to begin advancing on Vicksburg until 1 July, when the city was on the verge of surrender. After the town surrendered, Johnston was easily defeated by Sherman at the battle of Jackson.

Johnston was not blamed for the loss of Vicksburg, and was wisely retained in command. In December, after Bragg lost Chattanooga to Grant, Johnston was directed to take personal command of Bragg's demoralized Army of Tennessee. Johnston did a good job reorganizing the army, and wisely chose not to take the offensive against Grant's superior forces. Instead, he planned to wear the enemy down during a defensive campaign and then counterattack when the moment was right, much as Bragg had done at Chickamauga in September 1863.

When the spring 1864 campaign opened, Johnston was facing Sherman instead of Grant. He conducted a masterful defensive campaign, and skillfully opposed Sherman's every move. This strategy led to a victory at Kennesaw Mountain on June 27, but even so Johnston was unable to stop Sherman's advance and his broad flanking movements.

In July Sherman stood poised to attack Atlanta. Johnston's defensive strategy had kept his army intact, and he was now ready to man Atlanta's defenses. President Davis, however, had grown weary of Johnston's maneuvering and did not trust him to fight another battle. Fearing another Vicksburg, Davis fired Johnston and replaced him with the aggressive John Bell Hood. The move proved to be disastrous. Hood took the offensive as soon as he took command, and soon lost Atlanta. He then decided that the best way to stop Sherman's March to the Sea was to invade Tennessee. This strategy—quite the opposite of what Johnston would have advised—was also a disaster. While Sherman marched initially unopposed to Savannah, Hood smashed his army to pieces at Franklin and Nashville. In just six months Hood completely destroyed the Army of Tennessee.

In February 1865 General Robert E. Lee, now commander of all Confederate armies, returned Johnston to command of the Army of Tennessee, tacitly admitting Davis' error in firing Johnston the previous July. Rather than resign, as he well could have done, especially considering the poor size and condition of the army, Johnston obediently accepted his assignment. He did what he could to oppose Sherman's march through the Carolinas, hoping against hope to perhaps link up somewhere with Lee's army. The task proved futile against vastly superior Union numbers and resources.

Soon after Lee surrendered at Appomattox on 9 April, Johnston began negotiating with Sherman in North Carolina. Here he ran into his final confrontation with Davis. The Confederate president, fleeing South in haste, ordered Johnston to keep the war going. Johnston, though, saw that resistance was useless. He signed an armistice with Sherman on 16 April and surrendered on the 25th.

So ended the military career of one of the South's best but most misunderstood generals. Johnston's main problem was that he was cautions by nature, and so did not win the splashy victories that won attention. Instead, he ran three skillful defensive campaigns: in 1862 against McClellan in Virginia, in 1864 against Sherman in northern Georgia, and in 1865 against Sherman in the Carolinas. The significance of Johnston's performance in these campaigns was not fully appreciated at the time. In fact, the greatest praise for his work came from his opponents, Grant and Sherman, and from more recent military critics.

This is not to say that Johnston was without faults. He had good strategy, but at times lacked the ability to carry it out. He also was not a top level administrator, and so did not always have the confidence of his officers and devotion of his men. Simply put, his personality was not charismatic, and, competent as he was, he could be abrasive, particularly to the one man who counted most—President Davis. It was indeed unfortunate for the Confederacy that the personal differences between Johnston and Davis so directly affected Johnston's assignments and performance.

Johnston held a variety of jobs after the war. For several years he sold insurance in Savannah and then in Richmond. From 1879-1881 he served a term as a Virginia congressman in Washington. Later, from 1885-1891, he was a national commissioner of railroads. He did a great deal of writing to explain his wartime role, most notably in *Battles and Leaders of the Civil War* and in his autobiography *Narrative of Military Operations Directed During the Late War Between The States* (1874).

After the war, Johnston developed and maintained a close friendship with his one-time arch enemy, Union General William T. Sherman. Their relationship was so close that Johnston insisted on attending Sherman's funeral in February 1891, even though it was a cold and rainy day. The eighty-four-year-old general stood hatless in respect for his departed enemy, and in the process caught pneumonia. He died a month later, and was buried in Baltimore.

It was now the crisis of the battle. Grant worked desperately to stabilize McPherson's line, stiffened by a mass battery of 16 guns. Then he threw Brigadier General Marcellus Crocker's newly arrived division into the fray on McPherson's left. Grant's efforts worked. The Confederate attack ran out of steam 600 yards short of the Champion House, and Crocker's attack began to sweep them back up the hill. Pemberton saw his weary regiments began to break, and desperately ordered Loring to send help from the right. Loring sent two brigades, but they arrived too late to save the left. Their departure gave Loring too few men to

hold off McClernand's late attack, so after 1600 he too retired from the field. Through a critical error in judgment, he elected to retreat south rather than west because of the number of enemy troops in that direction. This move separated him from the rest of Pemberton's command, and to all intents and purposes took him out of the campaign when Grant moved up to close off Vicksburg.

Though receiving a deadly blast of canister in the face, Yankee soldiers successfully take an enemy battery at Champion's Hill.

Despite a powerful enemy counterattack, Grant's legion drives Pemberton's Confederate army from the field of Champion's Hill. The Federal victory here set the stage for the siege of Vicksburg.

Confederate Generals

The top Confederate officers in the campaign, J.E. Johnston and John Pemberton, were clearly outgeneraled by U.S. Grant and William T. Sherman, especially in the four weeks preceding the siege. Most of the division commanders at Vicksburg (the Confederates did not use corps structure) made a better showing.

The best Confederate division commander at Vicksburg was probably John S. Bowen. He was born in Georgia in 1830 and graduated from West Point in 1853. Bowen was the original colonel of the 1st Missouri Infantry 1861, and rose to command the 1st Missouri brigade in 1862. He was wounded at Shiloh, but returned in time to lead a division at Vicksburg. His gallant defense of Port Gibson on 1 May earned him a promotion to Major General. Though Bowen was a hard fighter, he was well aware of the futility of continuing to hold Vicksburg, and so had a key role in persuading Pemberton to surrender. He suffered so badly from dysentery during the siege that he died on 13 July, nine days after the surrender.

Another of Pemberton's top division commanders was Major General Carter L. Stevenson. He was born in Fredericksburg, Virginia, in 1817, and graduated near the bottom of the West Point Class of 1838. He began the war as Colonel of the 53rd Virginia Infantry. In 1862 he was promoted to Brigadier General and sent west to Tennessee. Here he served so well that he was promoted to Major General in October. He and his division were then sent from Chattanooga to reinforce Pemberton at Vicksburg.

Stevenson was exchanged soon after the surrender, and took command of his old division at Chattanooga, where he was on the losing side at the battle of Lookout Mountain.

Later in the war, Stevenson served at Atlanta, Franklin and Nashville, and Bentonville. He was throughout the war a Yeoman division commander who rose only briefly to temporary corps command in late 1864. He died in 1888 and was buried in Fredericksburg.

Martin L. Smith was another very competent division commander at Vicksburg. He was born in New York State in 1819 and graduated from West Point in 1842. He then entered the Engineer Corps and served with distinction in Mexico. When the Civil War broke out, he stayed with the South because of his personal inclinations and because his wife was from Georgia.

Early in the war Smith was Colonel of the 21st Louisiana Infantry. He rose to the rank of Major General in November 1862, and used his engineering experience to good stead when he supervised the preparation of Vicksburg's defenses that winter.

Smith was paroled in March 1864. Since there were no division commands available at the time, he became Chief Engineer for Robert E. Lee's Army of Northern Virginia. That summer he transferred to hold the same post in John B Hood's Army of the Tennessee at Atlanta. After Atlanta fell, he helped lay out the defenses of Mobile. Smith remained an engineer after the war. He died in Savannah in 1866.

John H. Forney was a division commander of average ability. He was born in North Carolina in 1829, and graduated from West Point in 1852. When the war broke out he was the original colonel of the 10th Alabama Infantry. He served in Virginia until March 1862, when he was promoted to Brigadier General and sent west. There he commanded the District of the Gulf for awhile before being promoted to Major General and receiving command of a division in Pemberton's command.

Forney was exchanged on 13 July, only 9 days after Vicksburg surrendered. In 1864 he commanded a division in Louisiana, and ended the War as commander of the District of Texas.

After the War, Forney ran a small military academy in Alabama. He died in 1902.

Forney's brother, William H. Forney, was a brigade commander in Lee's army. He was wounded 13 times during the War.

Pemberton's weakest division commander was W.W. Loring. He was born in North Carolina in 1818. Loring became an army officer before the war, but never attended West Point. At the start of the Civil War he was made Brigadier General in command of a small army in West Virginia. Here he had a run in with "Stonewall" Jackson, and was eventually transferred to Mississippi, where he received command of a corps.

Loring got the nickname "Old Blizzards" when his division was defending Fort Pemberton in the spring of 1863. When his troops bombarded the Union positions he would shout, "Give them blizzards, boys!'

Loring was accused by Pemberton of not following orders quickly enough to support the army's left flank during the battle of Champion Hill. At the close of the battle Loring made a poor decision to retreat south instead of east. This move separated him from the rest of Pemberton's command and kept him out of the Vicksburg siege.

Loring later rose to corps command in the Army of the Tennessee, and served at Atlanta and in the Carolinas.

After the war Loring spent several years as military advisor to the Khedive of Egypt. He died in New York in 1886.

Carter L. Stevenson.

John H. Forney.

William Loring.

J.S. Bowen.

The Battle of Champion's Hill (called Baker's Creek by the Confederates) was a close, hard fought fight that was decisive to the campaign. Pemberton to his dying day blamed the loss of the battle on Loring's failure to provide prompt support to the left when ordered, but the simple fact was that Pemberton had been outgeneraled by Grant tactically at the battle just as he was outmaneuvered strategically in the whole campaign. On his part, Grant was pleased to have won the battle, but was annoyed that McClernand's late attack had prevented him from destroying Pemberton's command completely and marching almost unopposed into Vicksburg.

The casualty lists were long for Champion's Hill. Grant lost 400 killed, 1800 wounded and 200 missing, a total of 2400, half of these in Hovey's division alone. Confederate losses were 400 killed, 1,000 wounded, and 2,400 missing (many of these were wounded) for a total of 3800, 70 percent of which were in Stevenson's division, that bore most of the fighting all day. These figures do not include over 5,000 men in Loring's division, lost to Pemberton for the rest of the campaign.

A Civil War battlefield after the fighting ended was a gruesome scene no matter which side won. One soldier from Illinois described Champion's Hill that evening: "All around us lay the dead and dying, amid the groans and cries of the wounded. Our surgeons came up quickly, and, taking possession of a farmhouse, converted it into a hospital, and we began carrying ours and the enemy's wounded to the surgeons. There they lay, the blue and gray intermingled; the same rich, young American blood floating out in little rivulets of crimson; each thinking he was in the right. With no anesthetic to soothe the agony, but gritting their teeth, they bore the pain of the knife and the saw, while arms and legs were being severed from their bodies."

Where Pemberton's hopes were crushed, the battlefield of Champion's Hill.

CHAPTER VIII

VICKSBURG: THE FIRST ASSAULTS

On the night of 16 May, Pemberton withdrew his shattered army to a position he had previously prepared in front of the Vicksburg and Jackson railroad bridge over the Big Black River. Here he placed Bowen's division in the forward trenches and allowed Stevenson's crippled division to go into reserve. He stayed up all night waiting for Loring's division to arrive to strengthen the line. Loring, though, did not come, since he had retreated south after Champion's Hill and was now cut off by Grant's army. Loring's absence left Pemberton's bridgehead position seriously undermanned, and Bowen's soldiers knew it. When they saw several Union divisions move up to attack them at 0800 on the 17th, the tired Confederates fired a few rounds and then began to bolt to the rear. Their retreat soon became a stampede. When it was over after an hour later, the Confederates had lost 18 cannons and 1,800 prisoners; Union losses were less than 300.

It was fortunate for Pemberton's army that someone during the hasty retreat on the 17th remembered to set fire to the railroad bridge over the Big Black River. This act gave the Confederates the rest of the day to make their retreat to Vicksburg unmolested while Grant's advance was stalled at the river. Grant began building two improvised bridges as soon as he reached the river, but they took until midnight to finish. There was only one pontoon bridge traveling with the army. It reached the scene in the early afternoon and was not ready for use until after dark.

Pemberton formed all his troops in the defenses of Vicksburg. There was not time to pull back the heavy cannons at Haynes' Bluff, so he ordered them to be spiked and the defenses blown up as thoroughly as possible. As his weary men reached Vicksburg, he posted Stevenson's divisions on the right, M.L. Smith's on the left, and Forney's division in the center of the lines; Bowen's veterans were held in reserve. These troops totaled just over 24,000 men, with 102 cannons. The previous week had been a disastrous one that reduced his strength by 40 percent with 6,000 battle casualties and the disappearance of Loring's division. Pemberton was nevertheless confident in his ability to defend the town. He had six weeks worth of provisions stored up, and ample ammunition, as long as it was not wasted.

Pemberton's confidence was buoyed even more when he surveyed the strength of Vicksburg's defenses. The river batteries had already proven their worth several times, and he had no reason to fear an enemy naval attack or landing. The landward defenses had never been tested, but were strongly built on the many hills that surrounded the city. They stretched for eight miles in an arc from Fort Hill, one-half mile north of Vicksburg, to South Fort, on the Mississippi three miles south of town. The Jackson Railroad and six roads that entered town were each guarded by a strong fort. Between the forts were continuous lines of ramparts and rifle pits, fronted by a ditch eight feet deep and fourteen-feet wide. Fields of fire had already been cleared for the defenses, and approaches were broken up with branches, logs, sharpened stakes and old telegraph wire.

Pemberton was just getting settled into Vicksburg on the afternoon of 18 May when he received a disconcerting message from Johnston, whose small force was in the area of Brownsville on Grant's northern flank: "If you are invested in Vicksburg, you must ultimately surrender. Under such circumstances, instead of losing

Demoralized, outnumbered and overwhelmed, Pemberton's command collapses at Big Black River in the face of a powerful Union attack.

both troops and place, we must if possible, save the troops. If it is not too late, evacuate Vicksburg and its dependencies, and march to the northeast."

Johnston's suggestion made strong sense from a purely military standpoint. But it conflicted directly with orders that Pemberton had from President Davis to hold Vicksburg and Port Hudson "at all costs." Faced with this dilemma, Pemberton called another council of war. Here he agreed with the opinion of his generals that leaving Vicksburg would destroy the army's morale. He was also swayed by an assurance from President Davis that relief would be sent if a siege developed. For these reasons he replied to Johnston: "I have decided to hold Vicksburg as long as possible, with the firm hope that the Government may yet be able to assist me in keeping this obstruction to the enemy's free navigation of the Mississippi. I still conceive it to be the most important point in the Confederacy."

Grant's divisions began reaching Vicksburg on the evening of 18 May, and continued arriving on the morning of the 19th. Grant assigned Sherman's corps the right of the line, with McPherson in the center and McClernand on the left. As they arrived, the troops were stunned by the strengths of the Confederate works. One officer observed: "A long line of high, rugged, irregular bluffs, clearly cut against the sky, crowned with cannon which

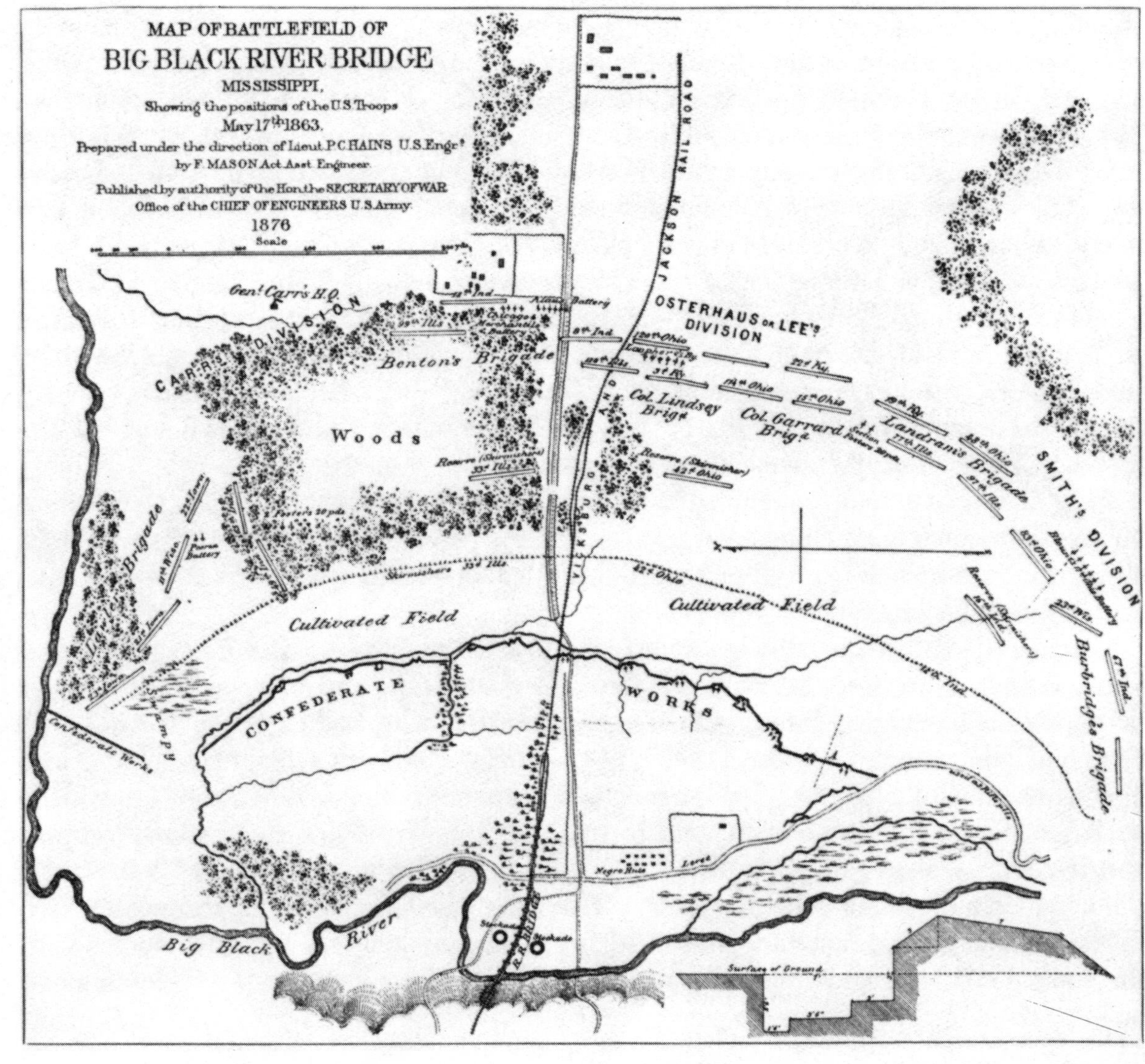

Remains of the Big Black River Bridge, burned in the wake of Pemberton's retreat.

Federal pontoon bridge across the Big Black River.

Grant meets with his subordinates to discuss his grand strategy for taking Vicksburg.

Believe It or Not — The Miraculous Bullet

The Battle of Raymond, Mississippi, was a minor affair fought on May 12 1863, during Grant's final drive on Vicksburg. The following anecdote concerning the battle was written with all sincerity by Dr. L.G. Capers, a Confederate surgeon during the war, in the 1874 issue of *The American Medical Weekly*:

On the 12th day of May, 1863, the battle of Raymond was fought. General Gregg's brigade met the advance of Grant's army, under General Logan, about one mile from the village of Raymond. About three hundred yards in rear of my regiment was situated a fine residence, the occupants being a matron, her two daughters, and servants, the host being absent in another army. About 3 o'clock P.M., when the battle was raging most furiously, the above-mentioned lady and her two daughters (aged respectively fifteen and seventeen), filled with interest and enthusiasm, stood bravely in front of their homestead, ready and eager to minister to their wounded countrymen should they fall in the dreadful fray.

Our men were fighting nobly, but pressed by superior numbers, had gradually fallen back to within one hundred and fifty yards of the house. My position being near my regiment, suddenly I beheld a noble, gallant young friend staggering closer, and then fall to the earth. In the same moment a piercing scream from the house reached my ear! I was soon by the side of the young man, and upon examination, found a compound fracture with extensive comminution of the left tibia; the ball having ricochetted from these parts, and in its onward flight, passed through the scrotum, carrying away the left testicle. Scarcely had I finished dressing the wounds of this poor fellow when the estimable matron came running to me in the greatest distress, begging me to go to one of her daughters, who, she informed me, had been badly wounded a few minutes before.

Hastening to the house, I found that the eldest of the young ladies had indeed received a most serious wound. A minie ball had penetrated the left abdominal parietes, about midway between the umbilicus and the anterior spinal process of the ilium, and was lost in the abdominal cavity, leaving a ragged wound behind. Believing there was little or no hope of recovery, I had only time to prescribe an anodyne, when our army fell back leaving both field and village in the hands of the enemy.

Having remained with my wounded at the village of Raymond, I had the opportunity of visiting the young lady the next day, and, interruptedly, for a period of nearly two months, at the end of which time she had entirely recovered, with no untoward symptoms during treatment; save a severe peritonitisis, she seemed as well as ever!

About six months after her recovery, the movements of our army brought me again to the village of Raymond, and I was again sent to see the young lady. She appeared in excellent spirits, but her abdomen had become enormously enlarged, so much so as to resemble pregnancy at the seventh or eighth month. Indeed, had I not known the family and the facts of the abdominal wound, I should have so pronounced the case. Under the above circumstances, I failed to give a positive diagnosis, determining to keep the case under surveillance.

This I did.

Just two hundred and seventy-eight days from the date of the receipt of the wound by the minie ball, I delivered of this young lady of a fine boy, weighing eight pounds. I was not very much surprised; but imagine the surprise and mortification of the young lady herself, her entire family. This can be better imagined than described. Although I found the hymen intact in my examination before delivery, I gave no credence to the earnest and oft-repeated assertions of the young lady of her innocence and virgin purity.

About three weeks from the date of this remarkable birth, I was called to see the child, the grandmother insisting there was "something wrong about the genitals." Examination revealed an enlarged, swollen, sensitive scrotum, containing on the right side of a hard, roughened substance, evidently foreign. I decided upon operating for its removal at once, and in so doing, extracted from the scrotum a minie ball, mashed and battered as if it had met in its flight some hard, unyielding substance.

To attempt to picture my astonishment would be impossible! What may already seem very plain to my readers, as they glance over this paper, was, to me, at the time, mysterious. It was only after several days and nights of sleepless reflections that a solution flashed before me, and ever since has appeared as clear as the noon-day sun!

"What is it?" The ball I took from the scrotum of the babe was the identical one which, on the 12th of May, shattered the tibia of my young friend, and in its mutilated condition, plunged through his testicle, carrying with it particles of semen and spermatozoa into the abdomen of the young lady, then through her left ovary, and into the uterus, in this manner impregnating her! There can be no other solution of the phenomenon! These convictions I expressed to the family, and, at their solicitations, visited my young soldier friend, laying the case fully before him in its proper light. At first, most naturally, he appeared skeptical, but concluded to visit the young mother. Whether convinced or not, he soon married her, ere the little boy had attained his fourth month.

As a matter of additional interest, I may mention having received a letter during the past year, reporting a happy married state and three children, but neither resembling, to the same marked degree, as the first—our hero—Pater familias.

Jefferson Davis and the Vicksburg Campaign

Confederate President Jefferson Davis had a special interest in the course of the Vicksburg Campaign, since he owned a plantation named "Brierfield" located 20 miles south of Vicksburg. He had spent 30 pleasant years here before the war, and expected to return to Brierfield when the war ended in Confederate victory. When he went to live in the President's mansion at Richmond, Davis left care of his plantation to his house slaves and to his brother, who lived next door at Hurricane Plantation.

In the summer of 1862 Union forces coming up the river from New Orleans burned Joseph Davis' Hurricane Plantation. The President's nearby plantation was not touched, though his slaves ran off. Because of this situation, Davis chose not to visit Brierfield during an inspection tour of Mississippi's defenses he took in December 1862. He did, however, visit his brother's new plantation near Bolton.

Davis' trusted Negro overseer, Ben Montgomery, took care of Brierfield and what was left of Hurricane Plantation during the winter of 1862-1863. He even managed to plant some crops and recover some of the livestock that had wandered off.

Any hopes Davis had of his plantation surviving the war unscathed were shattered in late May 1863 when Grant's troops thoroughly sacked his beloved home. The Yankees stole everything of value, and used their bayonets to rip up what they were not able to carry off. One unnamed soldier stole Davis' inscribed copy of the U.S. Constitution; it was found by the side of the road by Union General W.T. Sherman while he was on his way to the battle of Champion Hill on 16 May. Before departing Brierfield, the invading Union troops painted "This is the house that Jeff built" over the doorway. At least they did not burn the mansion down. Instead, they let a band of ex-slaves move into the house.

Davis was unable to return to Mississippi after the war because of his two year imprisonment and subsequent traveling abroad. He finally came home in 1875, but by then Brierfield had other owners. He ended up spending his days as guests of the owners of Beauvoir on the state's Gulf Coast. Davis liked the estate so much he purchased it in 1879 and wrote his memoirs there. He died at Beauvoir in 1889. The mansion is preserved today as a shrine maintained by the Sons of Confederate Veterans.

President of the Confederacy, Jefferson Davis with his wife.

peered ominously from embrasures to the right and left as far as the eye could see. Lines of heavy rifle-pits, surmounted with head logs, ran along the bluffs, connecting fort with fort, and filled with veteran infantry. . . . The approaches to this position were frightful—enough to appall the stoutest heart."

Grant was also awed by the defenses, but felt he might be able to carry them by an immediate direct assault because of the disorganized and demoralized condition of Pemberton's troops. For this reason he ordered an assault at 1400 on the 19th, before all his troops were up or in position. The attack was made principally by Sherman's troops, which had been the first to arrive the night before and so had had time to survey the ground. At the appointed signal, Frank Blair's division charged bravely forward at the part of the Confederate line near the Graveyard Road. The troops managed to reach the base of the Confederate works, but were pinned there and could proceed no farther. McPherson's supporting troops did not make it that far. They proceeded about 200 yards before their attack was stopped by the ravine in front of the Confederate lines. Farther to the left, McClernand was slow getting his men into position and did not contribute much at all to the assault.

At the height of the fighting, Sherman's 54th Illinois ran out of ammunition. The colonel called for volunteers to get a fresh supply. A 14-year-old drummer boy named Orion R. Howe offered his services, and was sent to the rear for .54 caliber bullets. On the way he was wounded in the leg, and then ran into General Sherman. Sherman suggested he get to a hospital, but the boy refused because he had to get the ammunition. Sherman told the boy not to worry, he would take care to send the ammunition forward. In the heat of battle, Sherman forgot to carry out his promise, which would not have mattered anyway since the boy had told him the wrong caliber of ammunition. In spite of this, Howe in 1896 received a Medal of Honor for his heroism.

The Confederate troops proved to be not quite as dispirited as Grant expected. They bravely stood their positions and fired as fast as they could, inflicting almost 1,000 casualties while losing less than 100 themselves. Not one Union soldier had breached their lines. Sherman summarized the attack briefly in his *Memoirs*: "My troops reached the top of the parapet, but could not cross over. The Rebel parapets were strongly manned, and the enemy fought

Rebels entrench themselves in the works before Vicksburg and prepare for a long, painful, and bloody siege.

William T. Sherman

William Tecumseh Sherman, Grant's right-hand man in the Vicksburg campaign, was born in Lancaster, Ohio, on 8 February of the year 1820. When his father, Judge Charles R. Sherman, died in 1829, young William was sent to live with the family of Senator Thomas Ewing of Ohio.

Sherman's foster father obtained for him an appointment to West Point in 1836. "Cump," as he was known to his friends, was a good student and graduated sixth of the 42 members of the class of 1840. Following several years of frontier duty in the 3rd Artillery, Sherman served on the staff of Captain Phil Kearny during the Mexican War. In 1850 he married his foster sister Ellen Ewing.

By 1853 Sherman found army service boring and unrewarding, so he resigned from the army. His first civilian job was as an agent in San Francisco for a St. Louis bank. When that bank went broke during the recession of 1857, he became a lawyer and real estate broker in Leavenworth, Kansas. Business connections brought him an appointment in October 1859 as superintendent of the new Louisiana State Seminary of Learning and Military Academy at Alexandria, Louisiana (the forerunner of today's Louisiana State University). When the Civil War began, Sherman was offered a commission in the Confederate Army. How different the war would have been had he accepted it! Instead he refused, resigned his post as superintendent, and signed up as president of a street car company in St. Louis!

As the Civil War became serious, Sherman was appointed colonel of the 13th U.S. Infantry. He commanded a brigade of U.S. Regulars at the battle of First Bull Run in July 1861, and fought so well in a losing cause that he was promoted to Brigadier General. He was given a brigade of volunteer troops, but proved so intolerant of their inexperience that he was transferred to Kentucky.

Sherman's high strung nature was at its worst during his brief tenure as commander of the Department of the Cumberland in the fall of 1862. He

continued to have no faith in the militia troops assigned to him. Then he began a long running feud with newspaper reporters, who accused him of being crazy. The pressure of his job did, in fact, cause Sherman to have the equivalent of what we would call today a nervous breakdown. He had no choice but to go on sick leave.

Fortunately for the Union, Sherman's health soon recovered enough for him to return to active duty. As luck would have it, he was assigned command of U.S. Grant's former post at Cairo, Illinois. He then became commander of a division of new troops in Grant's army, beginning a life long association with Grant that would benefit both generals. His troops were routed in the Confederate surprise attack at Shiloh, but Sherman fought so bravely (he was wounded) that he won national attention and a promotion to major general.

When Grant became commander of the Western armies, he sent Sherman to occupy Memphis. From Memphis, Sherman led an early expedition against Vicksburg and was defeated at Chickasaw Bluffs in December 1862. His troops were then absorbed into John McClernand's short lived Army of the Mississippi. Under McClernand Sherman played a key role in the capture of Arkansas Post in January 1863. In fact, Sherman may have planned the whole campaign, but this is hard to determine since the braggart McClernand took credit for all of it.

Sherman became commander of Grant's XV Corps when his mentor reorganized the Army of the Tennessee for his final drive on Vicksburg. Sherman fought ably and nobly throughout this campaign. After Vicksburg fell, he accompanied Grant to Chattanooga. This successful campaign brought Grant a promotion to commander of all U.S. armies. When Grant left to direct the war from Virginia, he assigned command of the western armies to his protege Sherman.

Sherman's first objective was to drive on Atlanta and capture that key Southern city. A long campaign, including a disastrous frontal assault at Kennesaw Mountain in June 1864, brought him finally to Atlanta, which fell after a siege and some bloody counterattacks by Confederate General John B. Hood. Sherman now determined to march on Savannah. His troops, though, had little difficulty living from their foraging as they "made Georgia howl" during their March to the Sea. The success of this campaign (Savannah fell in mid-December) played a key part in assuring President Lincoln's reelection that fall.

From Savannah, Sherman pursued Joe Johnston's Confederate Army northward. In the process he captured Charleston and then Columbia, South Carolina. Sherman caught Johnston in North Carolina, and forced him to surrender on April 17. He at first gave Johnston the same terms Grant gave Lee at Appomattox, but these terms were hardened by Secretary of War Stanton in the vengeful days following President Lincoln's assassination.

Sherman had a highly successful postwar career in the army. In 1866 he was promoted to lieutenant general as Grant's second in command. He then succeeded Grant as full general and commander in chief when Grant became president in 1869. He dealt successfully with the Indian campaigns and retired from the army in 1883. He died in New York City in February 1891. Sherman's memoirs, published in 1875, are an excellent account of the war.

hard and well. My loss was pretty heavy. . . . "

Grant spent the next two days bringing up the rest of his troops and establishing a new base of supply on the Yazoo River near the Chickasaw bluffs. He then ordered an all-out assault for the morning of Friday, 22 May. He and his corps commanders felt that the attack on the 19th had failed because it was hastily

After driving Pemberton into his trenches around Vicksburg, Grant established a supply base on the Yazoo to allow for the arrival of reinforcements, ammunition and other stores.

organized, was on too narrow a front, and had struck the strongest part of the enemy's works. Grant was also concerned about the size of Johnston's force in his rear, reported to be 20,000 and growing.

A pre-assault artillery bombardment was started at 0500 on the 22nd, supported by all of Porter's warships and gunboats in the river. It lasted a full five hours before the various infantry corps stepped off to their attack.

The first to attack was McClernand on the left. He was determined to win the glory of being the first to enter Vicksburg after the dishonor of losing his army command earlier in the year. McClernand's main attack focused on the Railroad Redoubt opposite the center of his line. Two regiments of Lawler's brigade rushed to the base of the fort, and a detachment of the 22nd Iowa broke into the fort through an opening made by the earlier artillery bombardment. In a sharp hand-to-hand fight the Iowans seized the fort and kept their flag flying over it all day. They were unable to proceed farther, however, even when reinforced by the 77th Illinois of Landram's brigade. Another Confederate fort on higher ground 100 yards behind the Railroad Redoubt made it too hazardous to advance.

On McClernand's left, Osterhaus' and Hovey's divisions came near the Confederate works, but they received such heavy fire from a square fort on their left that they had to halt. The troops on McClernand's right had more luck against the fort above the Baldwin's Ferry Road. They passed the ditch in front of the fort and put their flags on the parapet, but were unable to penetrate.

Newspaper reporter Sylvanus Cadwallader was a witness to McClernand's attack, and described it movingly as follows: "As McClernand's advance neared the rebel works, it came into plain view from my place of shelter. It had been so mercilessly torn to pieces by Confederate shot and shell that it had lost nearly all resemblance to a line of battle, or the formation of a storming column. Officers and men were rushing ahead pell-mell without much attention to alignment. The small number in sight could no longer be mown down by artillery, as the guns of the forts could not be depressed sufficiently. When they crossed the deep ditch in front of the earthworks and began to ascend the glacis, they were out of musketry range for the same reason. . . . A straggling line, continually growing thinner and weaker, finally reached the summit, when all who were not instantly shot down were literally pulled over the rebel breast works as prisoners. One stand of our colors was planted half way up the embank-

Grant's Horses

Like all Civil War generals, Grant owned a number of mounts that he used during the course of the war. A few achieved fame through their personality or length of use.

Grant's favorite horse in the early part of the War was Jack, a cream-colored animal he bought in his hometown of Galena, Illinois, when the war started. He used Jack principally as a spare mount, or for parades, until late 1863.

During the important 1862 campaigns of Fort Donelson and Shiloh, the General's primary horse was a roan named Fox. Grant obtained a new mount on the Shiloh battlefield when he found a run-down animal abandoned by the Confederates. The general, who was a lover of horses, nursed the animal back to good health and named him Kangaroo for his bobbing gait. Kangaroo was his favorite horse during the Vicksburg campaign. During this campaign he also acquired yet another mount. Jeff Davis was a black pony captured at the Mississippi plantation owned by Jefferson Davis' brother, Joseph.

Grant's favorite horse from late 1863 until the end of the war was a large (17 1/2 hands high) animal named Cincinnati which was given to him as a gift after the battle of Chattanooga. He permitted no one else to ride Cincinnati except President Lincoln on one occasion in 1865.

Grant with his favorite steed, Cincinnati.

Upon reaching Vicksburg, the Federals find a formidable network of trenches guarding the city. Despite many desperate assaults, only a siege would force the Confederates to capitulate.

ment and remained there until a daring Confederate ventured over and carried it back inside."

In the center, McPherson's attack also failed to achieve success. Due to the lay of the land, many of his troops were hit by a bad crossfire and could not reach the Confederate works. The farthest advance was made by Stevenson's brigade, which reached the ditch in front of the Great Redoubt. The 7th Missouri placed its colors on the redoubt's parapet, only to lose six standard bearers killed in a few minutes. The colors were left flying while the regiment kept to the shelter of the ditch. They were not retrieved until the end of the day.

The 22nd Iowa regiment breaks into Confederate entrenchments during an sanguinary assault on 22 May.

It was the same story with the attack at Sherman's end of the line. His assault was led by 150 volunteers who were to fill in the ditch at the Stockade Redan with poles and boards. They rushed forward at full speed until the Confederate defenders rose and fired their first volley en masse. Most of the storming party went down, their bodies clogging a narrow road and making it difficult for the next wave to advance. A few members of the first party, however, did make it to the ditch, and even managed to plant their flag on the Confederate parapet. It waved there all day despite Confederate attempts to rush forward and seize it.

About noon Grant and Sherman met for a conference. Sherman admitted that his assault had failed, and Grant replied that it was the same with McPherson and McClernand. During this conference, Grant received several dis-

Failing to take the town by direct attacks, Grant's men prepare for a long siege and build entrenchments.

patches from McClernand claiming that he was carrying the enemy works and needed support. Grant was skeptical of McClernand's success, since he had seen only a few Union flags reach the Confederate lines on McClernand's front. Nevertheless, he directed McPherson and Sherman to renew their attacks in McClernand's favor.

In response to McClernand's request for help, Grant sent Quinby's division to the left. When he arrived there, Quinby expected to be used in support of McClernand's attacks. Instead, McClernand sent Quinby in an unsupported attack on the Second Texas Lunette, hoping to relieve the pressure on his own troops at the Railroad Redoubt. Quinby's attack was repulsed in half an hour. Undeterred, McClernand ordered some of his own troops to make yet another attack. One colonel for a time refused to do so, arguing "No man can return from the charge alive!" Finally he gave in and went to the attack, to be killed in the first volley.

Meanwhile, Sherman had renewed his assault at 1500, and met no more success than he had earlier in the day. McPherson likewise committed fresh troops, only to see them mowed down in their charge. The few that could reach the enemy's lines had to seek cover in the ditch or behind any logs or natural cover available. Many were so pinned down by enemy fire that they could neither advance nor retreat until night came with its protecting darkness.

The day had indeed been a disastrous one, with 3,200 Union casualties compared to 500 for the Confederates. The attack was, in fact, the fourth worst Union assault of the war, ranking after Fredericksburg (13,000 casualties), Cold Harbor (7,000 casualties), and the Petersburg Crater (3,800 casualties).

The 23 May assault was also the beginning of the end for General McClernand. Both Sherman and Grant blamed his misleading dispatches for causing the second round of bloody attacks. Sherman complained "that General McClernand, instead of having taken any single point of the rebel main parapet, had only taken one or two small lunettes open to the rear, where his men were at the mercy of the rebels behind their main parapet, and most of them were actually thus captured." Grant also had had enough of the commander of the 13th Corps: "General McClernand's dispatches misled me as to the real state of the facts, and caused much of the loss. He is entirely unfit for the position of corps commander, both on the march and on the battlefield. Looking after his corps gives me more labor and infinitely more uneasiness than all the remainder of my department."

The General Nobody Liked: John A. McClernand

The Civil War had more political generals than all other wars put together. For awhile in 1861 and 1862 it seemed that anyone who was a senator or representative could get appointed to command a regiment or brigade, regardless of the level of his military experience (or total lack thereof). It is not surprising that these politicians-turned generals were responsible for a great number of casualties and lost battles. Prime examples are Confederate Brigadier General John B. Floyd at Fort Donelson, Union Major General Dan Sickles on the second day of Gettysburg, and Union Major General Nathaniel P. Banks in the 1862 Shenandoah Valley Campaign and later in the 1864 Red River Campaign. Fortunately for everyone involved, the rigors of field campaigns drove many elderly political generals into early retirement. Other political generals were shunted into unimportant war theaters or even fired because of their demonstrated inabilities. Among the latter was Major General John A. McClernand, one-time U.S. Congressman from Illinois and military rival to U.S. Grant.

John Alexander McClernand was born near Hardinsburg, Kentucky, on 30 May 1812. During his youth his family migrated across the Ohio River to Illinois. There he was trained as a lawyer, but found his true calling in politics. McClernand was a strong supporter of the Douglas wing of the Democratic Party. He served in his state legislature from 1836 to 1843 and in the National Congress from 1843 to 1861. He personally did not favor the abolitionists, but was against the secessionists.

McClernand did not at first take up arms when the war began. Instead, he showed his loyalty by helping to recruit soldiers and by advancing the cause of Illinois officers (one of his projects was lobbying successfully for U.S.Grant's promotion to Brigadier General). As an unofficial observer he accompanied the Illinois troops that occupied Cairo at the opening of the war. Back in Washington he sponsored resolutions to use all power necessary to restore U.S. authority in the South.

The despised John McClernand.

Lincoln showed his gratitude for McClernand's support as a war-Democrat by yielding to Illinois pressure to appoint McClernand a brigadier general. McClernand promptly accepted the job for its political prestige and because he held the Jacksonian belief that a real leader could lead in any activity simply by natural ability. In point of fact, McClernand had no military experience other than his brief service as a private in the Black Hawk War of 1832 (where Abraham Lincoln had served as a captain).

The new brigadier general promptly returned to Illinois and used his considerable influence to raise a full brigade of troops (over 4000 men). That fall, when his men were ready to take to the field, they were assigned to General Grant's command in Missouri. Their first combat came at the battle of Belmont, Missouri, on 7 November 1861. Here Grant made a successful riverine landing, but his first attacking wave was repulsed by defending Confederate troops. McClernand was sent in with the second wave and successfully repulsed the enemy. However, he then lost control of his men, who broke ranks to plunder the Confederate camp. This allowed the Confederates enough time to reform and counterattack, driving Grant's whole command back to the river. Despite his earlier mistake, McClernand showed great heroism during the battle. This brought him the attention of newspaper reporters, and McClernand relished their limelight.

During Grant's important spring 1862 campaign, McClernand was promoted to command of one of Grant's five divisions. It did not take long for his military inexperience and abrasive temperament to surface. When Fort Henry was captured on 6 February McClernand failed to move quickly enough to intercept its retreating garrison. In the ensuing battle at Fort Donelson, he lost a large number of men in an unauthorized attack on 12 February. To deflect his commander's wrath, McClernand sent his own report of the battle to his personal friends in Washington, exaggerating his own success and downplaying the role of the rest of the army.

McClernand pulled the same trick after the battle of Shiloh. Here Grant's army was routed by a Confederate attack on 6 April, only to counterattack and win the battle on the next day. McClernand fought bravely in the battle, though his division was smashed up on the first day. After the battle he wrote again to President Lincoln, criticizing Grant's generalship and claiming much of the credit for the victory.

Grant's response to this meddling was to assign McClernand a minor backwoods command at Jackson, Tennessee. McClernand understood the situation and promptly went on a leave of absence to Illinois and Washington, D.C. His goal was nothing less than to seek permission to raise a new army for the purpose of capturing Vicksburg!

McClernand's grandiose plans won the attention and then the approval of President Lincoln and Secretary of War Stanton. In late October, he returned to Illinois to begin raising his new army. (Once his Vicksburg plan was approved, McClernand dropped his machinations to replace George McClellan as Commander of the Army of the Potomac). Amazingly, McClernand raised over 40,000 men in less than a month.

It appears that Grant, the Union commander in western Tennessee, had no idea of McClernand's actions or intentions. Lincoln and Stanton chose not to inform Grant of McClernand's project! Instead, Grant first heard of it through Henry Halleck, the nominal commander of all U.S. armies. Halleck, too, had been kept in the dark concerning McClernand's plan. For this reason he was incensed, and joined forces with Grant to undercut McClernand.

Grant's plan was to boldly steal most of McClernand's troops and send them in an attack on Vicksburg under the command of General William T. Sherman. Sherman managed to spirit off 30,000 of McClernand's men while McClernand was busy getting remarried (he married the sister of his deceased first wife). Sherman's campaign, however, failed to meet success when he was repulsed just north of Vicksburg on 29 December.

When McClernand heard of what Grant and Sherman were doing, he exploded in anger. He rushed to Sherman's headquarters, took possession of what troops he could, and proclaimed them the Army of the Mississippi. However, instead of advancing against Vicksburg as he had announced, he went after easier prey at Arkansas Post. This lightly defended town was captured on 11 January.

McClernand's next goal was Little Rock, Arkansas. Grant, however, was growing impatient with McClernand's dallying in Arkansas. He and Halleck had finally persuaded Lincoln that McClernand was not a reliable commander. Grant also claims in his *Memoirs* that Sherman and Admiral Porter had written to him that they distrusted McClernand and felt he was unfit for command. Sherman later wrote of McClernand, "He was and is the meanest man we ever had in the West—with a mean and gnawing ambition, ready to destroy everybody who could cross his path. He would not give an order to renew the attack on his arrival, but was ever ready to throw on me the blame of failure."

On 12 January, Grant received permission from Washington to fire McClernand if necessary. He met with the general on 17 January and decided to disband the short lived Army of Mississippi and absorb it into his own Army of the Tennessee. McClernand was to be demoted to command of a corps (the 13th). He, of course, was full of resentment and furious at Grant, Sherman and Porter.

Looking back today, it certainly does not seem a good idea for Grant to have had such a disgruntled subordinate leading a major section of his army. Yet that is what happened. McClernand, true to form, groused constantly about Grant's lack of success moving against Vicksburg. He sent numerous letters to Washington complaining of Grant's drinking problems and faulty tactics. The main reason McClernand stayed with the army at this time was the hope that Grant would be fired so he himself would be able to take his rightful place as commander of the Army of Tennessee.

The feud between Grant and McClernand came to a head on the trenches before Vicksburg. McClernand's troops fought well during the final drive on Vicksburg, and McClernand, true to form, kept tooting his own horn. Grant, by now totally weary of his boastful subordinate, refused to give McClernand compliments even when they were due. This situation led McClernand to send reports of his fighting directly to northern newspapers. Sherman and McPherson took offense at McClernand's criticism of their efforts, particularly in the unsuccessful assaults of 19 and 22 May. They complained to Grant, and Grant also exploded, largely because McClernand had not cleared his reports through headquarters before sending them north. He got information of the facts of the incident, and relieved McClernand from command.

The unhappy general unsuccessfully sought a court of inquiry to clear his name. He had little choice but to fade into the background while Grant's star gleamed after the fall of Vicksburg. In early 1864 McClernand did wheedle command of some of Nathaniel P. Banks's troops during the Red River Campaign. However, there was little glory to be gained when this campaign failed miserably. McClernand ended up contracting a case of malaria, and went home for the rest of the war "awaiting orders."

After the war, McClernand returned to his first love, politics and law. His greatest success came when he was selected president of the 1876 Democratic National Convention (whose candidate, Samuel Tilden, lost the presidency to Rutherford B. Hayes by one electoral vote). General McClernand died in September of 1900, still wondering why it was that he failed to attain all the military and political glory that Lady Luck showered on his rival U.S. Grant.

SHERMAN AND VICKSBURG

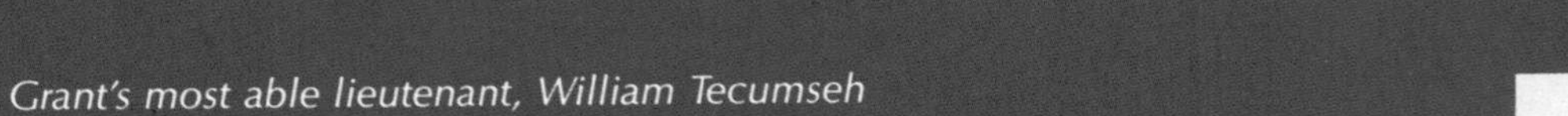

Grant's most able lieutenant, William Tecumseh Sherman.

Position of the 8th Michigan battery at Vicksburg.

BATTLE AT PORT HUDSON

Ships from Farragut's fleet engage the powerful batteries at Port Hudson.

The general charged to take Port Hudson, Nathaniel P. Banks.

BATTLE OF CHAMPION'S HILL

Joseph E Johnston.

John Pemberton.

The battle that culminated in the siege at Vicksburg, Champion's Hill.

VICKSBURG BESIEGED

Ulysses S. Grant

A bend in the majestic Mississippi River as seen from the Vicksburg entrenchments.

Grant surveys the extensive Federal and Confederate fortifications around Vicksburg. The city finally capitulated after 48 days of siege.

THE CRATER

The 45th Illinois leads the Federal charge into the crater left by the explosion of a mine dug under the Confederate entrenchments.

CHAPTER IX

THE SIEGE

The failure of Grant's 22 May assaults marked the beginning of the siege of Vicksburg, which is perhaps the most noted siege of the war. For over six weeks bad food, bad water and the searing sun of the Mississippi summer would torment the soldiers of both sides as well as the innocent citizens trapped inside Vicksburg. The siege was also a race against time as Pemberton tried to make his food and ammunition supplies hold out until relief could reach him while Grant strived to capture the fortress before Johnston's growing army at Jackson became too strong.

On 23 May, the day after the disastrous assaults, Grant began a two-day naval and land bombardment to keep the Confederate troops pinned down. He then began adjusting his lines. It was especially important to shift his troops to the left, for there was a two and one-half mile unoccupied stretch between McClernand's left and the river. This gap was not satisfactorily covered until Lauman's division of the 16th Corp arrived from Tennessee on 28 May.

One important detail remained unfinished from the 23 May assaults. Grant for two days declined Pemberton's offer to declare a truce in order to bury the dead and collect the Union wounded still lying on the field. Finally he consented to a two-hour cessation of hostilities to begin at 1800 on 25 May. Soldiers of both sides took this opportunity to fraternize, trade, play cards, and survey each other's trenches as they went about their gruesome work. Sergeant William Tunnard of the 3rd Louisiana, who left a very vivid account of the siege, described the scene that day: "Flags were displayed along both lines, and the troops thronged the breastworks, gaily chatting with each other, discussing the issues of the war, disputing over differences of opinion, losses in the fight, etc. Numbers of the Confederates accepted invitations to visit the enemy's lines, where they were hospitably entertained and warmly welcomed."

Grant at first believed the siege would last no more than a week. As May turned into June, he realized the siege might be a long one. He sent out a call for reinforcements from other departments, and set about pressing the siege as hard as he could. Altogether he had some twelve miles of trenches, which were daily pushed closer to the enemy works by saps or zigzag trenches that were out of the enemy's direct line of fire. Moveable gabions and other devices were improvised to offer cover for the front lines. Most effective of these was what was called a sap roller, constructed as follows: Two empty barrels were lashed together, one on top of the other, then wrapped round and round with willow saplings, filled with earth, covered and laid on its side Grant concentrated his approach on the several roads that entered the city, particularly the Stockade Redan in the north and the Great Redoubt and Railroad Redoubt in the center. The lines of approach were planned by engineers, but soon every Union soldier by experience and common sense was able to lay out new works. One Union soldier wrote: "Every man in the investing line became an army engineer day and night. The soldiers worked at digging narrow, zigzag approaches to the rebel works. Entrenchments, rifle pits, and dirt caves were made in every conceivable direction. When entrenchments were safe and finished, still others yet farther in advance were made, as if by magic, in a single night. Other zigzag underground saps and mines were made for explosion under forts. Everyday the regiments, foot by foot, yard by yard, approached nearer the strongly armed rebel works. The soldiers got so they bored like gophers and beavers, with a spade in one hand and a gun in the other."

Grant's lines started the siege some 600 yards

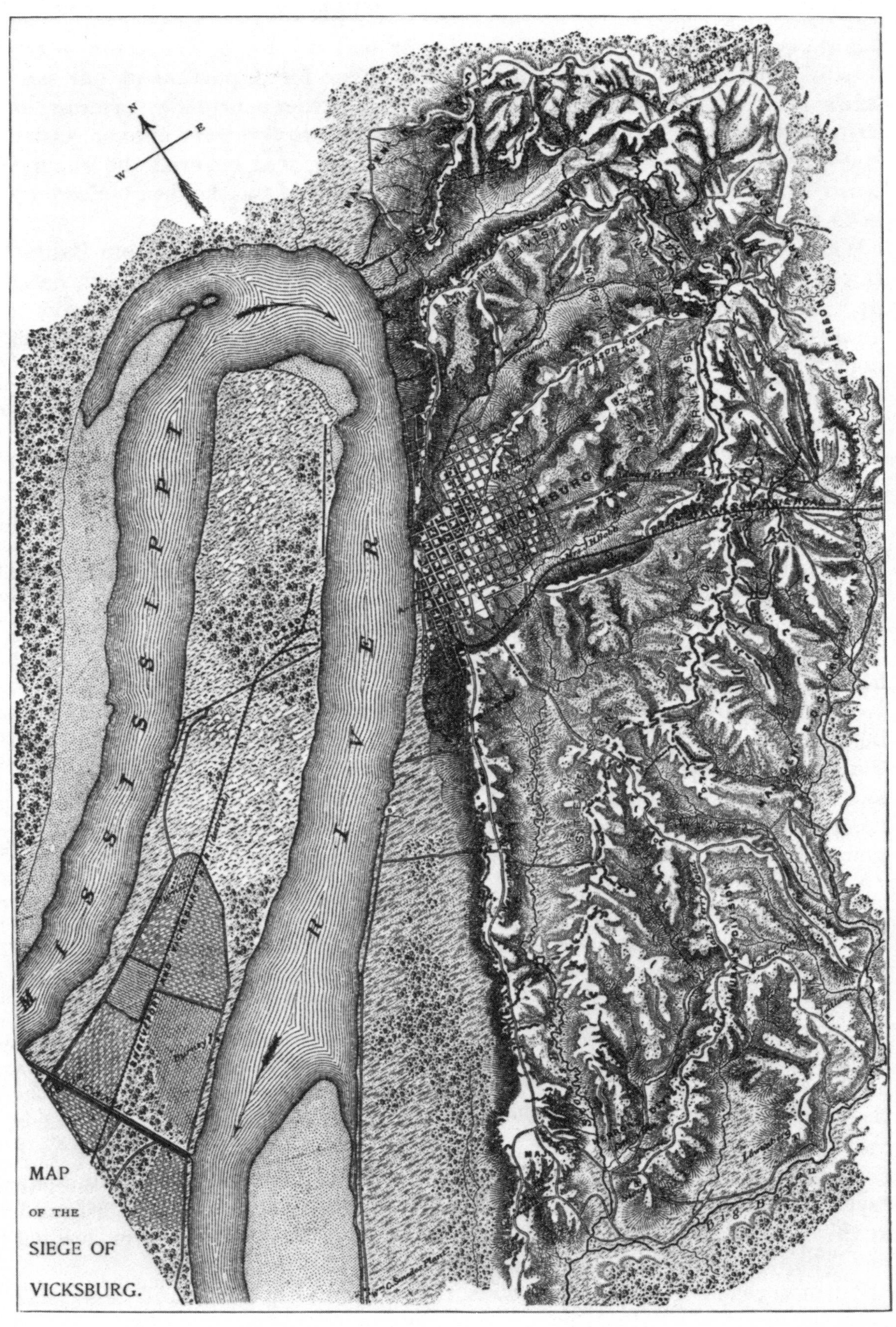

MAP OF THE SIEGE OF VICKSBURG.

A powerful assortment of guns guard the Mississippi from Federal use at Vicksburg.

Federals constructing gabions for their defenses.

Siege Songs

The lack of provisions in besieged Vicksburg might have led her Confederate defenders to extreme despondency. Instead, they held on, buoyed by wry humor they expressed in song. One such song ended as follows:

Swear, boys, swear Vicksburg
shall ne'er surrender,
Swear, boys, swear that not
one vandal foe
Shall tread her soil while
one arm can defend her
Unless her rations
get damnation low.

The most tuneful chorus among the Confederate defenders of Vicksburg was the glee club of the 3rd Louisiana Infantry (the same outfit that was blasted by the Union mine detonated on 25 June). Captain J. H. Jones of the 38th Mississippi noted that the 3rd Louisiana "also had a sort of poet who would compose songs adapted to popular melodies which the club would sing. These songs were sometimes humorous, often satirical, but more commonly sad and sung in a minor key."

The poet spoken of by Captain Jones was probably Private A. Dalsheimer of the 3rd Louisiana. Private Dalsheimer composed the following song to the tune of "Life on the Ocean Wave":

Life On The Vicksburg Bluff

A life on the Vicksburg bluff,
A home in the trenches deep,
Where we dodge Yank shells enough,
And our old pea bread won't keep.

On old Logan's beef I pine,
For there's fat on his bones no more;
Oh, give me some pork and brine,
And tuck from the Sutler's store.

The bullets may whistle by,
The terrible bombs come down;
But give me full rations, and I
Will stay in my hole in the ground.

A life on the Vicksburg bluff,
A home in the trenches deep,
Where we dodge Yank shells enough,
And our old pea bread won't keep.

During the siege one clever gentleman in Vicksburg made up the following verses for the still popular tune, "Listen to the Mockingbird." To appreciate it, we need to recall that a "Parrot" was a kind of Union rifled cannon named after its inventor, Robert P. Parrot:

'Twas at the siege of Vicksburg,
of Vicksburg, of Vicksburg,
'Twas at the siege of Vicksburg,
When the Parrot shells were
whistling through the air.
Listen to the Parrot shells,
listen to the Parrot shells,
the Parrot shells are whistling through
the air.

from the Confederate works. As the Union lines were pushed forward, they came within 100 yards of the enemy lines—sometimes even ten or twenty—by the end of June. At these close distances, soldiers in the front lines had to be very careful to guard themselves against ever present enemy sharpshooters. Sometimes troops raised a cap on a ramrod above their works just to see how long it would take for it to be hit, or they would take bets on how often it would be struck in a certain time span.

One Union major was amazed at the techniques and effectiveness of some Indian sharpshooters in the 14th Wisconsin. On 3 June he wrote, "These Indians had fixed their heads with leaves in such a way that you could not tell them. They would creep on their bellies a little distance, then keep quiet, then move ahead until they could get the position they were after, which was generally a log, behind which they could lie without very much exposure. They silenced the rebel cannon in front almost entirely."

Coonskin's tower overlooking the Confederate works. From this position, the plucky gunner drew a bead on unfortunate enemy troops who exposed themselves.

One of the most noted Union sharpshooters was 2nd Lieutenant Henry C. Foster of the 23rd Indiana Infantry, fondly known as "Coonskin" by his fellows in Logan's division, of the 17th Corps. Coonskin (named for his Davy Crockett cap) liked to creep toward the Confederate line during the night and burrow into the ground with just a peephole showing. When daylight came he would then leisurely pepper away at the enemy. Sometimes he took a supply of food and water with him, and would hold his gopher hole for several days.

Coonskin's most famous deed was to build a small tower from rails and ties taken from the Vicksburg railroad. His tower was bulletproof, and soon reached a level above the height of the Confederate lines. This enabled him to pick off individual enemy soldiers at will, so causing great consternation to the Confederates.

Soldiers in such close quarters, strangely enough, at times developed bonds with their enemies across the trenches. Exchange of newspapers, and small items of trade was not unusual during truces or when officers were looking the other way. At one point midway through the siege, a Missouri soldier in Bowen's Confederate division saw a Missouri flag in the Union lines. Boldly he went forward during a lull in the picket firing, and unscathed, inquired to see if he knew any of the Missouri Yankees. Soon a number of soldiers from both armies were meeting to swap tales and trade food and coffee for Confederate tobacco. After the fraternizing was over, men returned to their lines and to business, "shooting at each other's heads with all the eagerness of sportsmen."

At another time, Captain Henry S. Nourse of the 55th Illinois was approached on the picket line by a fellow from Mississippi. The Confederate "inquired for the whereabouts of the 54th Ohio, and being told that the 54th men were our particular friends and near neighbors, asked that Sergeant ? of that regiment, if alive, might be notified to come to the picket line at a certain hour the next night, where he would recover something of great value to him. The sergeant was found, and appearing as requested, received from the Southerner a letter enclosing the likeness of his sweetheart, which he had lost somehow during the battle of Shiloh."

Besides the ever present danger from bullets

A Yankee lieutenant colonel takes time off from his duties to take a shot at the enemy works.

Snipers exchange shots during the siege. This activity made most in the front lines think twice about exposing themselves to deadly enemy fire.

and shells, the soldiers on both sides had to endure bad water and heat that topped 100 degrees Fahrenheit. Another great hazard was posed by hordes of bugs and insects that caused all kinds of diseases. Brigadier General W.W. Orme of Herron's Union division wrote, "This is an awful hot country here full of bugs of all sorts. I am now suffering terribly from the effects of mosquitoes and other bugs. I am full of bites all over. There is a small insect about the size of a pin's point which bites its way into the flesh and makes a very sore place. This insect is called a 'chigger' or 'jigger.' We all are suffering from its depredations. They are much worse that the 'wood tick.' I have to stop after every sentence I write to scratch myself and drive off the bugs."

Strange But True - Four Stories of the Campaign

Private George H. Higgins of the 99th Illinois (Carr's division, 13th Corps) received the Medal of Honor for boldly advancing his company's flag right up to the Confederate works after his regiment's color-sergeant was killed during the bloody Union assaults on the morning of 22 May. What is unusual is that part of the documentation that brought Higgins his medal in 1898 was written by a Confederate soldier, from Texas, Charles I. Evans. Evans' account reads as follows:

> After a most terrific cannonading of two hours, during which the very earth rocked and pulsated like a thing of life, the head of the charging column appeared above the brow of the hill, about 100 yards in front of the breastworks, and, as line after line of blow came in sight over the hill, it presented the grandest spectacle the eye of a soldier ever beheld. The Texans were prepared to meet it, however, for in addition to our Springfield rifles, each man was provided with five additional smooth bore muskets, charged with buck and ball.
>
> When the first line was within fifty paces of the works, the order to fire ran along the trenches, and was responded to as from one gun. As fast as practiced hands could gather them up, one after another, the muskets were brought to bear. The blue lines vanished amid fearful slaughter. There was a cessation in the firing. And behold, through the pall of smoke which enshrouded the field, a Union flag could be seen approaching.
>
> As the smoke was slightly lifted by a breeze, one soldier advanced, bravely bearing the flag towards the breast works. At least a hundred men took deliberate aim at him, and fired at point blank range, but he never faltered. Stumbling over the bodies of his fallen comrades, he continued to advance. Suddenly, as if with one impulse, every Confederate soldier within sight of the Union color bearer seemed to be seized with the idea that the man ought not to be shot down like a dog. A hundred men dropped their guns at the same time; each of them seized his nearest neighbor by the arm and yelled to him: "Don't shoot at that brave man again. He is too brave to be killed that way." When he instantly discovered that his neighbor was yelling the same thing at him. As soon as they all understood one another, a hundred old hats and caps went up into the air, their wearers yelling at the top of their voices: "Come on, Yank, Come on!"
>
> He did come, and was taken by the hand and pulled over the breastworks, and when it was discovered that he was not even scratched, a hundred Texans wrung his hands and congratulated

The soldiers on both sides were also kept awake by the Union artillery, which conducted intermittent bombardments from both the land and naval guns. The big guns were also fired randomly at night to keep the Confederates tense. Grant's army had an overwhelming preponderance of artillery and ammunition, with 220 cannons, not counting those on Porter's boats. Nor does this total include numerous makeshift mortars that were improvised at the front. Since the opposing lines were so close, Union artillerymen noted they were having difficulty hitting Confederate troops inside their defenses. For this reason they fashioned makeshift "coehorn mortars" by hollowing out sections of tree trunks and bracing them with circular iron bands. These homemade mortars worked very well to lob six-inch twelve-pound shells in an arc over and into the Confederate lines.

The Confederate defenders had only 102 cannons, less than half of Grant's total. Their heaviest pieces were some siege and naval guns in the river batteries. Two of these achieved special fame. Whistling Dick was a 18-pound smoothbore cannon whose bore had been rifled to give it greater range. This rifling gave the cannon's projectiles a peculiar whistling sound, and so named the cannon. Whistling Dick caused the Yankees great annoyance during the siege, most notably when it sank the gunboat *Cincinnati* on 27 May. After the war a cannon thought to be Whistling Dick was set up with other trophies at West Point. In the 1950's it was proved not to be the real Whistling Dick, but instead the Widow Blakely, another famous Confederate cannon in the siege of Vicksburg.

The Widow Blakely was a 7.44-inch rifled cannon, so named because it was the only piece of its type in the Vicksburg defenses. This cannon lost the tip of its barrel when one of its own shells burst prematurely during a fight with Union gunboats on 22 May 1863. The barrel was then trimmed at the break, and the piece was used as a mortar for the rest of the battle. Apparently, its Union captors were confused about him upon his miraculous escape from death.

(Higgins went to a prison camp until he was exchanged. He then served until discharged at the end of the war.)

* * *

On 20 June, soldiers of the 3rd Louisiana Infantry stationed in the "Great Redoubt" near the Jackson Road were astonished to see a Union soldier pop his head above the edge of their fortifications. Apparently this soldier got the notion of walking up to the Confederate fort—only 100 or so yards from the Union positions—and see for himself what was inside. It is hard to tell whether this guy was exceptionally brave or exceptionally foolish. Whichever was the case, he did not live to tell of his exploit. A Confederate defender of the Great Redoubt shot the enterprising Yankee dead the moment he peered into the fort.

* * *

Since the troops on both sides at Port Hudson were entrenched and were protected sniper fire became a deadly game. At one point in the siege Colonel Sidney Bean of the 4th Wisconsin felt the urge to shoot an enemy, so he made his way to an advanced rifle pit. When no enemies were in view, he became impatient and stood up to get a better view. A corporal warned him to stay down but it was too late. The Colonel was struck dead by a bullet through the brain.

* * *

At least one of the 77,000 Union soldiers who served at Vicksburg was a woman dressed as a man. This soldier was Albert Cashier, a 19 year old private in Company G, 95th Illinois. Cashier fought at Vicksburg, the Red River Campaign, and Nashville, without having her true sex discovered, and even passed a doctor's exam in 1899 to secure an army pension! She apparently lived her entire post-war life as a man. Her femininity was not discovered until she was hospitalized following a car accident in 1911, 46 years after the war. One of her comrades, Harry Weaver, wrote about Cashier in 1914 to help her keep her pension: "When we were examined at induction, we were not stripped. All we showed were our hands and feet. We never saw Cashier use the latrine. He was of very retiring position and did not take part in any games. He would sit around and watch, but would not take part. He had very small hands and feet. He was the smallest man in the company."

Cashier's real name, it turned out, was Jennie Hodgers. She was born in Ireland on Christmas day 1844. Why she enlisted and served as a man was never exactly determined, for she was close to senility when her ruse was discovered in 1911. A special examining board upheld her pension in 1913, but her weakness of mind led her to be committed to an insane asylum. She died in 1915 and received a full military funeral.

Occasional instances keep surfacing of women who served in disguise in the War. Most enlisted to be with a husband or family member; they were sent home as soon as their identity was discovered. One sergeant in the 10th New York Heavy Artillery served until she had a baby boy on March 6, 1865. Private Franklin Thompson (Sarah E.E. Seelye) served in the 2nd Michigan Infantry from 1861 to 1863 until she was disabled from malaria, when she left the army to become a nurse. We will never know exactly how many disguised women carried muskets in the war. Cashier is the best documented case to have served out her entire term of enlistment undetected.

The deadliest cannon in the Confederate arsenal at Vicksburg, Whistling Dick. The ammunition of this 18-pound rifled smoothbore gave off a distinct screech when fired, hence the name.

its name, and mislabeled it Whistling Dick when it was taken to West Point after the war. When the piece was properly recognized as the Widow Blakely in the 1950s, it was returned to Vicksburg National Military Park, where it can be seen today. Whatever happened to the real Whistling Dick cannot be determined. It was probably melted down and sold for scrap.

As the siege dragged on, Grant became so tense and bored that he went on a two-day drinking binge (see sidebar). Then at mid-month he lost his temper completely with General McClernand, who had been a thorn in his side for months. It seems that McClernand had sent to a newspaper a congratulatory order that gave himself and his troops all the credit for Grant's successes after the end of April. This article was seen first by Sherman and McPherson, who were still furious at McClernand for his role in uselessly extending the fruitless and bloody attacks on 22 May. When the two generals showed the congratulatory letter to Grant, he was enraged that it had not been cleared through him first, as procedure required. McClernand clearly had not done this because the article was so full of selfserving falsehoods. It was the last straw for Grant. He fired McClernand on 18 June and sent him back to Illinois. Grant appointed his friend Major General E.O.C. Ord to take McClernand's place as commander of the 13th Corps, where he served Grant well here and in Virginia until the end of the war.

Grant's Drinking Problem

Major General Ulysses S. Grant, the Union commander in chief at Vicksburg, had a reputation for being a drunkard that dogged him throughout his military career. The problem first appeared in the early 1850s when he was on garrison duty on the West Coast. Hard drinking was a common habit of officers on boring frontier duty. Grant, lonely for his wife and anxious that his military career seemed to be going nowhere. Recent studies suggest that Grant was not a heavy drinker; rather, he could not "hold his liquor well" and so was adversely affected by just a few drinks. This drinking problem was allegedly the reason he had to resign from the army in 1854.

Rumors of Grant's drinking problem surfaced again in early 1862. Reportedly he was drinking during moments of tension and boredom during the campaign against Forts Henry and Donelson. Critics of Grant claimed he was drinking and partying at Savannah, Tennessee, when his army was surprised and routed on April 6, 1862, at Pittsburg Landing, nine miles south of Savannah. The Union high command chose to overlook these accusations largely because Grant managed to win the battle of Shiloh on 7 April, and the Union had a dire need for winning generals.

One of Grant's sharpest critics was Matt Halstead, the editor of the *Cincinnati Commercial*. His low opinion of the general can be seen in a letter Halstead wrote to his friend Salmon P. Chase, Lincoln's secretary of the treasury: "You do once in a while, don't you, say a word to the President, or Stanton, or Halleck, about the conduct of the war? Well, now, for God's sake, say that General Grant, entrusted with our greatest army, is a jackass in the original package. He is a poor stick sober, and he is most of the time more than half drunk, and much of the time idiotically drunk . . . "

Grant's chief of staff, Lieutenant Colonel John A. Rawlings, was well aware of Grant's fondness for drink. Midway through the Vicksburg campaign, he made Grant promise to stay on the wagon until the campaign was over. Two months later he had to remind Grant of his promise to stay dry: "The great solitude I feel for the safety of this army leads me to mention what I had hoped never again to do, the subject of your drinking. . . . I find you where the wine bottle has just been emptied, in company with those who drink and urge you to do likewise. . . . [I beg you not] to touch a single drop of any kind of liquor no matter by whom asked or under what circumstances." Otherwise, Rawlings would resign. Grant for awhile kept his pledge to Rawlings to stay off the bottle. However, the boredom and stress of the siege led him to return to his old habits. Details of what exactly happened are unclear, but evidence indicates that Grant went on a drinking spree on 6-7 June 1863, while purportedly on an inspection trip up the Yazoo River.

The main source for the events of this trip is Sylvanus Cadwallader, a reporter for the *Chicago Times* who happened to be aboard the boat Grant was traveling on. Grant in his autobiography, of course, does not mention any drinking on the trip, and Grant's staff members kept silent about it for a long time out of loyalty to their boss.

Cadwallader claims that Grant was intoxicated early in his trip: "I was not long in perceiving that Grant had been drinking heavily, and that he was still keeping it up. He made several trips to the bar room of the boat in a short time, and became stupid in his speech and staggering in gait. This was the first time he had shown symptoms of intoxication in my presence, and I was greatly alarmed by his condition, which was fast becoming worse."

Cadwallader became so concerned about Grant's condition that he tried to get his staff members to take the general to his room. Failing at this, Cadwallader managed to bring Grant to the reporter's room. There the general "commenced throwing bottles of whiskey which stood on the table, through the windows, over the guards into the river." As Grant raged, Cadwallader urged, "I was the best friend he had in the Army of the Tennessee, that I was doing for him what I hoped someone would do for me, should I ever be in his condition . . . as it was a very hot day and the stateroom almost suffocating, I insisted on his taking off his coat, vest and boots, and lying down in one of the berths. After much resistance, I succeeded, and soon fanned him to sleep."

During the night, Grant woke up in a stupor and ordered his boat to put in ashore at a small town named Satartia. Cadwallader and a staff officer did not think this was a good idea, so they persuaded the staggering general to go back to sleep. Grant stumbled back to bed, and the boat turned around to return to Haynes' Bluff near Vicksburg.

Cadwallader thought the affair was over, only to find that morning that "Grant had procured another supply of whiskey from onshore and was quite as much intoxicated as the day before." Cadwallader tried to sober the general up, only to see Grant's boat dock that evening next to a steamer where a full blown party was on. Grant, of course, had to head for the party and take a few drinks.

Grant now decided to return to his headquarters near Vicksburg. Mounted on a impetuous horse named Kangaroo, he raced away from the river until he could ride no more. He then lay down in the grass and went to sleep with his saddle as a pillow. Cadwallader, who had followed Grant, sent for Grant's chief of staff, Lieutenant Colonel John A. Rawlins. Rawlins sent an ambulance to convey the general the remaining distance to his headquarters.

When the ambulance arrived at Grant's headquarters, Cadwallader was astounded to see Grant walk nonchalantly to bed. "He shrugged his shoulders, pulled down his vest, shook himself together, and as one just rising from a nap, and seeing Rawlins and Riggin, bid them good-night in a natural tone and manner, and started to his tent as steadily as he ever walked in his life."

Cadwallader continues, "My surprise nearly amounted to stupefaction. I turned to Rawlins and said I was afraid that he would think I was the man who had been drunk. But he replied . . . 'I know him. I want you to tell me the exact facts—and all of them—without concealment. I have a right to know them, and I will know them.' The whole appearance of the man intoxicated a fierceness that would have torn me a thousand pieces had he considered me to blame."

It is interesting to note that Grant appears to have had the ability to recover quickly from the adverse effects of too much drink. No less a figure than General William T. Sherman wrote in 1887: "We all knew at the time that General Grant would occasionally drink too much. He always encouraged me to talk to him frankly of this and other things and I always noticed that he could with an hour's sleep, wake up perfectly sober and bright. And when anything was pending, he was invariably abstinent of drink."

The next day was an awkward one. Grant never mentioned what happened (perhaps he didn't remember very much). Cadwallader wisely chose not to mention the trip, and was later rewarded with exceptional privileges and travel arrangements at Grant's headquarters.

Cadwallader decided to keep quiet about Grant's drinking spree until he wrote his memoirs in 1896. This long silence and lack of corroboration of the incident by other sources led Grant's defenders, historian Kenneth P. Williams and grandson U.S. Grant III to accuse Cadwallader of lying, when the reporter's journal was finally published in 1955.

Historian Dan Bauer in 1988 weighed all the evidence on Grant's alleged drinking binge, and sided with Cadwallader. Bauer cited as support for Cadwallader's story an account written by Charles A. Dana in his memoirs. Dana, who was named assistant secretary of war in 1863-1864, had been sent by the high command in Washington to keep a personal eye on Grant. Dana wrote that Grant on the boat trip to Satartia "was ill and went to bed soon after he started." For the rest of the trip, the general was too sick to make any decisions. "The next morning Grant came out to breakfast fresh as a rose, clean shirt and all, quite himself. 'Well, Mr.Dana,' he said, 'I suppose we are at Satartia now.' 'No, General,' I said, 'We are at Haynes' Bluff.' And I told him what had happened."

Bauer interpreted Dana's reference to Grant's "illness" on the Satartia trip to be a veiled reference to the drinking bout described by Cadwallader. This interpretation is sustained by a 1887 newspaper article published anonymously, but probably authored by Dana: "General Grant's seasons of intoxication were not only infrequent, occurring once in three of four months, but he always chose a time when the gratification of his appetite for drink would not interfere with any important movement that had to be directed or attested to by him."

The article continues, perhaps defending Grant a bit too much: "It was a dull period in the campaign. The siege of Vicksburg was progressing . . . [Grant] wound up by going on board a steamer which he had ordered for an excursion up the Yazoo River, and getting as stupidly drunk as the immortal nature of man would allow. But the next day he came out fresh as a rose, without any trace or indication of the spree he had passed through. . . . Grant got drunk on two or three other occasions, but the times were chosen with perfect judgment, and when it was all over, no outsider would have suspected that such things had been."

Bauer and recent Grant biographer William S. McFeely agree that Grant's drinking spree was deliberately covered up by those who knew about it out of a genuine fear that news of the binge might have caused Grant to be fired and replaced, perhaps by the conniving General John McClernand. Grant's immediate staff members kept quiet out of loyalty to the general, and Rawlings, weighing what was at stake, chose to keep silent despite the pledges he had extracted from Grant earlier in the campaign. Charles Dana, the administration's spy on Grant, also chose to keep quiet, at least until 25 years later. So did Grant's right hand man, William T. Sherman, who appears to have learned of the affair. Cadwallader bought into the coverup, even though disclosures would have been a news scoop of the first magnitude. The reporter later wrote, "My confidence in the military ability of General Grant had become so great by this time that I was unwilling to jeopardize his reputation in public opinion by adding anything to the rumors and stories in circulation concerning his inebriety."

It is indeed interesting to speculate what might have happened had word reached Lincoln of Grant's drinking binge on 6-7 June 1863. Grant's occasional slips with the bottle did not affect his performance at Vicksburg, but this incident, blown up by an enemy such as Matt Halstead, might have severely undercut Grant's support in Washington during the critical time of the Vicksburg siege.

CHAPTER X

THE VICKSBURG MINE

Given the closeness of the opposing lines and the very hilly terrain at Vicksburg, it is not surprising that enterprising Yankee engineers determined to dig a tunnel (or mine) under Confederate lines in an attempt to blow them up. The objective chosen for the mine was a strong Confederate position guarding the main Jackson Road. It was garrisoned by the 3rd Louisiana Infantry of Hebert's brigade, Forney's division, and so was known as the 3rd Louisiana Redan or the Great Redoubt. The lines opposing the 3rd Louisiana Redan were held by Leggett's brigade of Logan's division, 17th Corps. The center of their position was on a hill occupied by a large frame plantation house owned by the Shirley family (this remarkable house was struck numerous times by musket and cannon fire, but still stands today.) On 23 May Leggett's men started digging a zigzag approach trench that began 150 feet southeast of the White House (as the troops called the Shirley home). From here it snaked towards the Confederate line 400 yards to the west. The Union troops labored in 150 man shifts day and night in their sap or approach trench. Other troops were assigned to gather wood and make gabions and fascines to protect the diggers. Gabions were large cylindrical baskets of brush, while fascines were long bundles of bound brush. These were placed next to new positions and could be covered with dirt in order to shield troops from incoming fire.

The best progress in advancing the sap took place under the cover of darkness. Day workers were engaged primarily at deepening and widening the trenches dug the previous night. While work took place, skirmishers were actively employed to pin down enemy sharpshooters and marksmen.

The cause of building the sap was greatly improved on 25 May when the Confederates asked for a truce in order to bury the dead who had fallen between the lines during the fighting on 22 May. Union engineers took advantage of the truce to mingle with the burial parties and check out the lay of the land over which their sap needed to advance. As a direct result of this reconnaissance, the besiegers erected a post called Battery Hickenlooper on the highest spot between the White House and the Confederate lines. The fort, located about 130 yards east of the 3rd Louisiana Redan, would provide excellent covering fire for the Union troops working on the sap.

A sap roller such as those used for protection by Federal engineers as they dug trenches close to Confederate lines.

One of the more powerful Federal artillery positions before Vicksburg, Battery Sherman.

Federal troops dug into position at Vicksburg. Nearby was the fort occupied by the 3rd Louisiana which would be the object of the Grant's first mining attempt.

Even more support was offered by a battery of two 8-inch naval guns set up just southeast of Battery Hickenlooper. These monsters caused the Confederates a great deal of anxiety because they could easily silence the Rebel guns only 100 yards distant. A Confederate defender of the Great Redoubt wrote: "These terrible missiles, with their heavy scream and tremendous explosion, somewhat startled the boys, being a new and unexpected feature in the siege, and necessarily increasing the already accumulated dangers of their situation. After knocking the breastworks to pieces, and exhibiting their force and power, the enemy commenced a systematic method of practice, so to make the shells deadly missiles of destruction. So skillful and expert did they soon become in handling these huge siege pieces, that they loaded them with powder, producing force sufficient to only propel the shells over the breastworks, and they rolled among the men, producing a general scramble to escape the force and danger of their explosion."

An entrenched Federal battery prepares to unleash its deadly load upon the enemy's position.

Construction of the sap west of Battery Hickenlooper was aided greatly a kind of saproller. This consisted of a wicker casing easily ten feet long and five feet in diameter, filled completely with cotton. Its purpose was to protect the diggers from flanking fire while they worked. The Confederates, of course, thoroughly hated this moving shield. One wrote that it "became a perfect annoyance to the regiment, and various plans were proposed for its destruction . . . Some of the men actually proposed to make a raid on it, and set it afire, a plan which would have been the height of madness."

Instead of attacking the saproller head on, one Confederate thought up a better way to destroy it. Lieutenant Colonel Samuel I. Russell of the 3rd Louisiana found that "fire bullets" could be made by stuffing bits of cotton soaked in turpentine into the hollow base of the minie ball bullet; the explosion of the firing would ignite the cotton and send the fiery missile to its destruction.

Russell's invention appeared to be a failure when he tested it on 9 June: "Procuring turpentine and cotton, he filled the ball with the latter, thoroughly saturated with the former. A rifle was loaded, and, amid the utmost curiosity and interest, fired at the hated object. The sharp report was followed by the glittering ball, as it sped from the breastworks straight to the dark mass of cotton-balls, like the rapid flight of a fire-fly. Another and another blazing missile was sent on the mission of destruction, with apparently no satisfactory results, and the attempt was abandoned amid a general disappointment."

This disappointment changed to exultation a couple hours later when the saproller burst into flames. Apparently the cotton had smoldered for quite awhile after it was struck by the fire bullet. Needless to say, the sight of the blazing sap-roller "was a source of general satisfaction and rejoicing." The Union sappers were all the more disheartened at the loss of their guardian because they could not understand how it had been set afire. They did not learn what Lieutenant Colonel Russel had done until they talked to Confederate prisoners after Vicksburg had surrendered.

The burning of this saproller was only a temporary setback for the Yankee besiegers. In a few days they built a new, improved saproller that was encased entirely in wicker so that it would not catch fire as easily. Using this new saproller, the Union sappers made good progress over the next two weeks, advancing their sap by night and widening and deepening it during the day.

The Confederate defenders found themselves frustrated trying to check the relentless advance of the Union sap. Once the Yankees got close to the Confederate works, the defenders found that they could not aim their rifles without standing up and providing a clear target themselves to the enemy. Since their artillery pieces were checked by the powerful Union naval guns near Battery Hickenlooper, the Confederates really had only one good defensive weapon: to roll shells with lighted fuses downhill in front of the Union troop positions.

It was at this stage of the siege that both sides began experimenting with primitive hand grenades. One grenade commonly used by the Confederates consisted of "an iron shell weighing roughly a pound, shaped like a hen's egg, and filled with powder. From one end projected a rudder of feathers, from the other a percussion rod was held extended by a spring. When the shell was hurled at the enemy, the tail feathers kept the nose of the missile forward so that, on striking the target, the rod sprang back and struck a cap to detonate the powder."

Miners digging a tunnel under the Confederate entrenchments.

Victim of Whistling Dick, the Cincinnati. After being sunk in the waters near Vicksburg, the ship was later salvaged and refurbished.

On 22 June, the sap reached the base of the hill occupied by the 3rd Louisiana Redan. Engineers now called forward 336 soldiers with coal mining experience to dig the actual mine that tunneled under the Confederate position. The miners were organized and led by two commanders, Lieutenant Russell of the 7th Missouri and Sergeant Morris of the 32nd Ohio. The men worked six at a time in one hour shifts: two men chipped with pickaxes, two men shoveled dirt, and two men removed sacks filled with newly dug earth. The tunnel constructed was four feet wide and five feet high. Work progressed quickly and easily because the local red clay was solid and readily cut and removed. By late June the tunnel was under the Confederate fort.

The Confederates were aware of the tunnel because they could hear the noise of the digging. They immediately began counter-mines, digging shafts that they hoped would intercept the Union mine. For awhile on 25 June the Yankee miners had to stop working because they were so near a Confederate counter-mine that they could hear enemy voices.

On 25 June the mine and two short side tunnels were filled with 88 25-pound backs of gunpowder, a total of 2,200 pounds of explosive force. For the sake of safety (and in case one fuse did not work), a total of six fuses were run back to the mouth of the mine. The mine was then packed with dirt bags, so that the force of the coming explosion would be directed upwards instead of down the mine tunnel.

The mine was set to be exploded at 1300 on 25 June. Thousands of Union troops were formed in the saps near Battery Hickenlooper to exploit the break in the Confederate lines that would be formed by the explosion. Captain Hickenlooper noted, "as far as the eye could reach, to the right and left, could be seen the long winding columns of blue moving to their assigned positions behind the besiegers' works. Gradually as the hour of three approached, the booming of artillery and incessant rattle of musketry, which had been going on day and night for thirty days, suddenly subsided and a deathlike and oppressive stillness pervaded the whole command. Every eye was riveted upon that huge redoubt standing above the adjoining works."

Finally the mine went off at about 1530. Captain Hickenlooper observed the spectacle. "At the appointed moment it appeared as though the whole fort and connecting outworks commenced an outward movement, gradually breaking into fragments and growing less bulky in appearance, until it looked like an immense fountain of finely pulverized earth, mingled with flashes of fire and clouds of smoke, through which could occasionally be caught glimpses of some dark objects—men, gun carriages, shelters etc." Another Union officer observed: "The burst was terrific. For a few seconds the air was filled with dirt, dust, stockades, gabions, timbers, one or two gun carriages, and an immense surging white cloud of smoke which fairly rose to the heavens, and gradually widened out and dissipated."

The blast, powerful as it was, was not as destructive as it might have been. The shape of the Union mine blew the center of the Confederate fort sky high, but did not make a wide breach; the resulting crater was about 50 feet across and 12 feet deep. Nor did the defending Confederates suffer heavy casualties. Union activity in the previous hours had made it clear what was about to happen. For this reason most of the Confederate defenders had been withdrawn to a newly constructed line of works immediately behind the 3rd Louisiana Redan. Altogether perhaps 100 Confederates were killed in the explosion. Six of these were members of a Mississippi regiment who were working in the countermine.

Over a ton of powder explodes beneath the redan occupied by the 3rd Louisiana during Grant's first attempt to break the Confederate lines with a mine.

The Prohibition General

Brigadier General Neal Dow, who commanded T.W. Sherman's First Brigade at Port Hudson, was well known throughout the country before the war as a leader of the prohibition (temperance) movement. He was born in Maine in 1804 and raised in a Quaker family. Early in life he began his one-man crusade against liquor. His speeches on the subject were printed in newspapers all across the country, and he was the sponsor of the Maine Law of 1851 that banned liquor there.

When the war began, Dow volunteered for service even though he was 57 years old. He felt it was his duty to help rid the country of slavery—abolition was another of his causes. Ironically, he found himself expelled from the Quaker Church because of his military service.

Dow was appointed colonel of the 13th Maine Infantry, which became known as the Temperance Regiment. He did not allow liquor in his camp, and did all he could to protect his men from the sins of the ordinary soldier—swearing, gambling, loose women, etc. Most of his troops tolerated his narrow-minded behavior, though more than a few hated him. Others delighted at slipping liquor into his lemonade or punch when he was not looking.

Dow was promoted to brigade command in the Department of the South in October 1862. While at this post he had a running battle with loose-living Ben Butler, Nathaniel Banks' predecessor as commander in New Orleans. At this time Dow also got into some trouble himself for his personal policy of confiscating anything he wanted from any Southerner, be he Confederate or pro-Union.

Dow was not feeling well when he led his brigade in a charge across Slaughter's Field at Port Hudson on the afternoon of 27 May 1863. He was complaining of a headache, and he personally thought the attack he was undertaking was totally insane. As he rode into battle, Confederate Colonel T.G. Reid of the 12th Arkansas ordered a number of his men to fire at Dow until he fell. Reid later wrote to

Neal Dow.

Dow, "It was a picture never to be erased from my mind, when about three hundred yards from my position I saw you fall or lean down your horse's neck, and a number of hospital corps ran and lifted you from your horse."

Dow's wound turned out to be only a slight one—a spent musket ball had struck him in the arm and raised quite a welt. He refused to go to the rear, and continued to advance with his men. He went only a short distance before he was hit in the left thigh by a rifle ball. This time he had to go to the rear. His surgeon Major S.C. Gordon was well aware of the general's stand against whiskey, so he refused to give him any liquor or chloroform to dull the pain as he treated his wound.

General Dow's travail was far from over. He went to a nearby plantation to recover, and his wound healed well. He should have gone to New Orleans to recuperate, but he harbored hopes of succeeding to command of T.W. Sherman's division, so he stayed as close as he could to Banks' army. In late June he kept hearing rumors that Confederate guerrillas were looking to capture him, perhaps inspired by Colonel John S. Mosby's capture of Union General Edwin Stoughton in his bed in Virginia on 8 March 1863. These rumors influenced Dow to move his quarters on 30 June 1863.

Ironically, Confederate cavalry commanded by Captain John McKowen, Jr., of the 1st Louisiana came to capture Dow right after he left his refuge. They were quite disappointed to hear that they had just missed their quarry. As they were leaving the plantation, though, the Confederates had a singular piece of luck—they ran right into General Dow, who had ridden back alone to pick up a few possessions he left behind.

General Dow was in Confederate prisons for eight months. Six of these were spent in notorious Lobby Prison in Richmond, and the last two in nicer quarters in Mobile, Alabama. Dow was surprised to find that he was quite a celebrity, even in prison. He was permitted to receive friends and guests, and was even permitted to give his famous temperance speeches. In March 1864 he was finally exchanged for none other than Brigadier General W.M.F.("Rooney") Lee, son of the Confederate Robert E. Lee.

Dow was bothered by his wounds so much that he had to retire from the army on 30 November 1864. He then continued his prohibition campaign, and even garnered 10,000 votes when he ran for U.S. President on the Prohibition ticket in 1880. He died in Portland, Maine, in 1897 and was buried there.

Port Hudson—The Siege

Banks' severe repulse at Port Hudson on 27 May taught him the same lesson Grant had learned at Vicksburg a few days earlier—the Confederate forces, even though greatly outnumbered, were not going to be readily dislodged from prepared fortifications. Consequently, Banks settled down on 28 May to a siege, angry and embarrassed that he had not made short work of the place and that he was prevented from marching triumphantly to Grant's aid at Vicksburg.

Banks was faced with a command problem. Heavy loss of officers on 27 May—particularly Generals Dow and Sherman—forced him to reorganize his high command. Brigadier General Cuvier Grover was put in charge of the right wing, consisting of his own and Paine's division, plus Weitzel's brigade of Augur's division. Brigadier General William Dwight took charge of Sherman's division, posted in the left wing. The center was held by Major General Christopher C. Augur and his division. Altogether Banks had almost 30,000 men available for the siege, but he claimed to have had only 20,000 in the field. The rest were scattered in garrisons and depots all the way back to New Orleans. Disease and guards against the Confederate cavalry further reduced his field force to less than 14,000 in the trenches. It should also be noted that over half of his men were new or untried in battle, and many of these were nine 9-months recruits whose term of service was set to expire that summer.

Setting up the siege also proved more challenging than Banks at first expected. As the troops dug trenches and created embrasures and salients, he had to arrange for a communications system to be set up. The terrain was too rough to use runners, so he and his signal corps established platform stations from which they could wig-wag messages around the lines and to Farragut's naval force. These stations and all rearward areas had to be guarded against forays from Gardner's cavalry force of around 1500 men. These men, commanded by Colonel John L. Logan were not en-

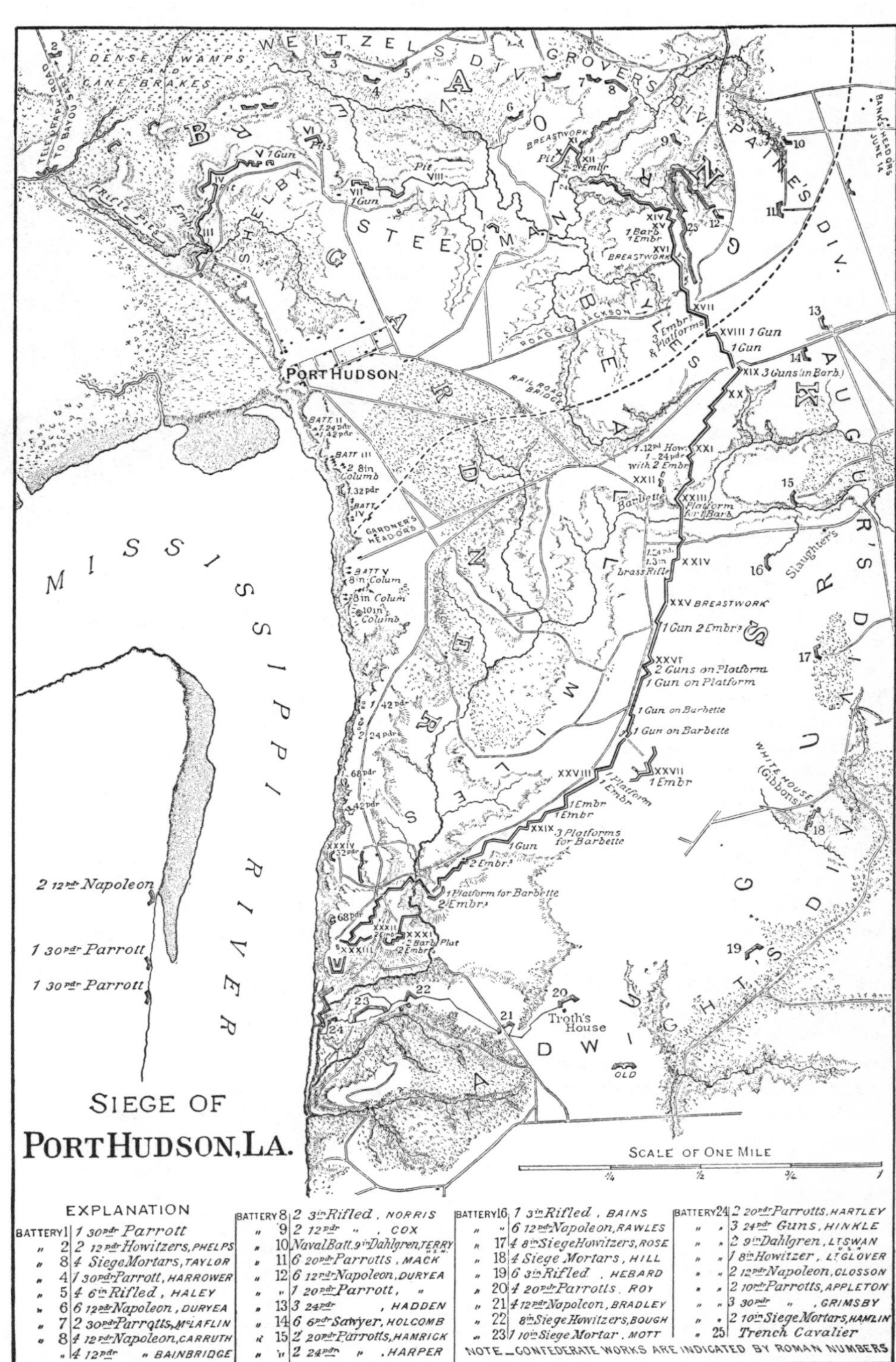

closed in the Port Hudson works, but instead were roaming loose in the countryside. They proved to be so much an annoyance to Banks that he had to deploy a fair portion of his troops outside his siege lines in order to guard against their mounted raids.

It did not take Banks long to realize that his principal opponent at Port Hudson was not Gardner's Confederates, but the sultry and oppressive weather. Banks' assistant Adjutant General, Lieutenant Colonel Richard B. Irwin later described how unbearable it was: "The heat, especially in the trenches, became almost insupportable, the stenches quite so, the brooks dried up, the creek lost itself in the pestilential swamp, the springs gave out, and the river fell, exposing to the tropical sun a wide margin of festering ooze." The humidity became terrible, making it difficult to move or even breathe. Then there were the bugs and disease. Conditions were equally terrible for the soldiers on both sides, the besiegers and the besieged.

Where the other siege took place, Federal fortifications at Port Hudson.

Fortunately for many of the Yankee soldiers, much of the labor to construct the siege works was provided by impressed Negro workers. Banks' engineers figured that the best way to overcome Port Hudson's defenses was to erect heavy batteries as close as possible to them and then blast the Confederates out. Embrasures were erected using piles of captured cotton (of which there was a great abundance) covered with dirt. Rifle pits were then dug nearby to house the infantrymen needed to guard the cannons from Confederate forays. To keep the troops from getting bored, they were put on rotations, digging three days in the trenches and then spending one day in the rifle pits.

No matter how close the Yankee guns came to the Confederate lines, they still were not able to blast the enemy into submission. The Confederate earthworks were simply too thick. Yankee shells embedded themselves in the earth without doing any real harm. In fact, it was usually more dangerous to be in the Confederate rear areas than in the front lines. Many Union cannons overshot their targets, with the result that their missiles caused much havoc on the buildings in Port Hudson and other rear line areas. These overshoots sometimes even did a slight service for the Confederate cooks by killing penned animals held by the commissary department. After a Union bombardment, the cooks often would not have to pick which animals to slaughter for dinner. They just carved up ones already slain by errant Union shells.

While the Yankees appeared to have endless guns and a limitless supply of ammunition, the Confederates were hard pressed to keep their few cannons in service. Temporary repairs had to be made constantly to keep vents and breaches open or repair broken wheels and carriages. When ammunition ran low, the Confederates shot anything that would fit down a cannon barrel—old bayonets, wrenches, scrap iron, old horseshoes, nails, broken bottles, and even chain links and pieces of wood. Even so, the Confederates often had to hold their fire except at crucial moments, in order to conserve powder and ammunition. Occasionally guns were moved to new positions in order to confuse the Yankees; sometimes fake guns made of painted logs ("Quaker guns") were also set up to draw enemy fire.

The Confederates had about 60 guns in their fortifications. The heaviest of these were posted on the bluffs overlooking the river. One of the biggest guns was a 10-inch Columbiad known affectionately as "Old Demoralizer." This big gun set off loud vibrations each time it was fired, and its sound varied greatly depending on its ammunition—sometimes its blast would sound like a beehive, other times like a train. Its worst sound, though, was the terrible screeching it made when it was rotated on its pivot carriage. Its ungreased iron tracks gave off sounds the likes of which no one had ever heard before. The most noted Confederate gun was a monster in the northern end of the lines called Whistling Dick. Its crew had the ability to strike squarely just about any target they set their sights on.

Altogether Banks had some 116 cannons,not including the numerous naval guns in Porter's river fleet. Thus the Union cannons completely surrounded the Confederate lines at Port Hudson. This also had the disadvantage that shots that were fired too high or too long were likely to go clear over the enemy works and land on Union lines beyond. One of the most effective Union batteries was one consisting of two 30-pounder Parrott rifles located on the west side of the Mississippi. The fire from these guns was so accurate that they could pick off the heavy guns of the Confederate river batteries one by one (the Confederates, though, did a good job of repairing these guns as best they could).

Quite often Union guns from anywhere in the line would fire at irregular intervals during the night just to keep the Confederates from sleeping. One would think that this tactic would have had the same effect on the Union troops!

As the siege dragged on, Banks was ready to try anything to bring the affair to a successful conclusion. On 13 June he decided to blast the town with a cannonade and then demand its surrender. The bombardment began at 1115, and an impressive affair it was! The cannonade lasted exactly one hour, whereupon it abruptly ceased. Banks then sent Gardner a note "formally demanding the surrender of the garrison of Port Hudson." Gardner chuckled because Banks' great bombardment had caused little damage and was not about to cow him into surrendering. The Confederate general's response was short and sweet: "Sir: Your note of this date has just been handed to me, and in reply I have to state that my duty requires me to defend this position, and, therefore, I decline to surrender."

Having failed to take the fortress by bombardment or negotiation, Banks decided to try another direct assault. His plan was to strike with his left and center at dawn on 14 June, the day after his failed cannonade.

Things did not go well from the start. The pre-attack artillery bombardment went off too early, at 0245. When it finished it was too dark for the infantry to advance. Even after the sun came up, a heavy fog mixed with cannon smoke made it difficult to see.

A massive 100-Parrot rifle bombards Port Hudson.

These 9-inch Dahlgren cannons were borrowed from a gunboat, but served just as well on land.

On the left, the troops from Dwight's division were assigned the task of taking the Confederate position called The Citadel at the extreme southern tip of the enemy line. At first Dwight's men got lost getting into position, delaying their attack. When they finally reached the Confederate lines, they found a huge ditch so full of abattis and sharpened sticks that it was impossible to cross. Wave after wave of brave Union troops assaulted the Confederate works, but could make no headway.

Union General Cuvier Grover had more detailed plans for his attack on the Confederate center, where he was ordered to strike the position known as the Priest Cap. Grover arranged his attack in waves, each with a specific role or mission. The first wave consisted of five companies of grenadiers who were to throw makeshift grenades (shells with sort fuses) into the Confederate works. When the grenades scattered the Southern defenders, seven regiments of infantry were to scale the Confederate position and hold it. Meanwhile four hundred picked men were assigned to fill in the deep ditch in front of the Rebel works with cotton bags. This would enable Paine's remaining infantry (three brigades) to charge right into Port Hudson. Finally, fifty black soldiers carried axes and picks to level the Confederate fortifications so that Nims' 2nd Massachusetts battery could accompany the advance.

Paine's attack, well planned as it was, was in trouble before it started. The preparatory artillery bombardment from 0300-0330 was finished too early, when it was still too dark to begin the assault. Any defenders who were scattered by the barrage simply returned to their positions, warned now that an attack was coming. Then, as Paine's men moved forward the ground they had to cover was much rougher and full of brush than they

The aftermath of Banks' 14 June attack on Port Hudson. Under a flag of truce, Federal dead and wounded are collected for burial or care.

had anticipated. But the worst blow to the attack came when General Paine, who was in the front lines directing the attack, was badly wounded in the leg. His loss took much of the steam out of the Union attack before it even started.

A few troops were undeterred by the loss of their commander. Some Wisconsin men of the first wave went over the Confederate works, only to fall casualty. The second wave met more success, as one Mississippi defender observed: "About one hundred of the bravest men I ever met came over our works. Here we had a hand-to-hand fight with the butts of our guns, the officers using their swords." The timely arrival of Confederate reserves then made quick work of the Yankee attackers in a short vicious fight.

This initial charge was the greatest success met by Paine's attack. Farther down the line everything became unraveled. Most of the improvised grenade bombs did not go off, even when the Confederate defenders picked them up and tossed them back. Due to the rough terrain, and heavy fire, several regiments were unable to advance within 30 yards of the Confederate line. The cotton carriers became disorganized when their flag went down, and instead of advancing, they used their burdens to construct hasty breastworks. Thus Paine's unsupported attack was a dismal failure even before the sun came up.

The supporting attack on Paine's right got off to a late start and then encountered one of the worst fiascoes of the war. Colonel Willoughby Babcock had noted the weakness of the Confederate position at Fort Desperate. He found an easy avenue of approach, and had everything all set to make a successful assault. But it seems that the engineers ordered to lay out the line of attack mistook the location of Fort Desperate and instead led the troops against the Priest Cap. Thus Babcock found himself assaulting one of the strongest Confederate works at Port Hudson instead of the well researched position he thought he would be attacking. The north side of the Priest Cap, where Babcock was to approach, consisted of a steep hill with a deep ditch in front, full of sharpened logs and raked by artillery fire.

Babcock's assault was scheduled to be made in the darkness at the same time as Paine's to his left. However, he was held up when a key supporting regiment, the 12th Connecticut, failed to come up and could not be located. Finally orders came for the attack to proceed without the Connecticut troops. By then it was 0500, long after Paine had been repulsed. Worse yet, it was now bright daylight.

The Yankee attackers were not optimistic about their chances of success, and could be fed into the attack only one regiment at a time because of a bottleneck in the approach route. This

Part of Port Hudson's almost impregnable works, the Citadel.

caused them to be mowed down before they could gain any momentum. The few brave lads who pushed forward found themselves stymied by the six-foot ditch in front of the Confederate works. Thus regiment after regiment attacked, stalled, and broke. Colonel Babcock went down with a wound in the leg. About 1000 Colonel Richard E. Holcomb had his brigade into the fray. Soon he fell dead. When General Banks sent an order to continue the attacks and "force an entrance at once into the Rebel works at all hazards," the impertinent reply came back from someone that "if the commanding general wanted to take the place, he should come up and take it himself."

Many battered Yankees spent the rest of the day simply holding on to whatever cover they had dived under. They were not able to retreat until the friendly cover of darkness descended. This bloody day saw almost 2000 casualties out of 8000 engaged. Banks' uncoordinated attacks had struck two of the strongest Confederate positions, the Citadel and the Priest Cap, and had been easily defeated with minimal losses by the defenders.

One would think that Banks would have learned his lesson after two bloody repulses. Instead, he determined to raise a band of 1000 picked men, nicknamed the Forlorn Hope, for use in a grand charge to carry the Confederate lines wherever a weak spot could be located and exploited. It took a few days to raise the force, which was then kept in constant state of preparation to attack on a moment's notice.

Meanwhile the siege dragged on and on and on. The heat, snakes, bad water and disease were equally bad on the attackers and the defenders. What affected the Confederates worst was a food shortage. They had started with sufficient food reserves to last for months. But a few lucky Union shots during the bombardment of 9 June set fire to several warehouses. All that was left was peas, corn on the cob, old molasses, and a lot of cows. Soon the cows ran out, so mules were substituted. When the mules ran out, the hungry defenders took to roasting dogs and even (if a few stray sources are to be believed) rats.

Banks' engineers contrived all sorts of battlements to advance the siege. Their efforts were aided by sheer Yankee ingenuity using building supplies at hand. Saps or covered trenches and walkways criss crossed the Union lines. Makeshift towers were built to give sharpshooters better shots at the defenders. At one point Engineer Captain John Palfrey designed what was called a trench cavalier, a truncated pyramid made of barrels and sand bags. This structure rose up for 15 feet and dominated the entire Confederate front opposed to it.

The most noted Union work during the siege was the Great Cotton Bale Battery erected in late June on General Dwight's front. Here the Yankees erected a great embrasure of cotton bales large enough to hold seventeen heavy guns. It took over a week to build and was even equipped with a spotting tower. The Confederates opposite the battery were so amazed at its construction that they didn't even maintain a harassing fire against it.

At last the Great Cotton Bale Battery was ready to go into action. It was 1545 on Friday 26 June. The air was filled with thunder and reverberations as the 17 guns blasted at the Confederate lines. But things did not work out for the Yankees as they expected. The concentration of guns in the battery gave the Confederates a target they could not miss. To make matters worse, the guns created so much smoke that their spotters could not see to aim their shots. This same smoke cloud also confused Farragut's mortar boats on the river, which had joined in the cannonade. Many of the mortars overshot their targets and exploded their shells on the besieging Union troops. It turned out that the mortars caused more Union casualties on that one day than they did Confederate losses in the whole siege.

One of the strangest events of the siege occurred on the night of 30 June, when the ever active Confederate cavalry (which was not entrapped by the siege but instead was roaming loose behind the Union lines) managed to capture Union Brigadier General Neal Dow while he was recovering from his 27 May battle wound at a plantation near Port Hudson. This act greatly disturbed General Banks, who substantially increased the size of his headquarters guard lest he be captured by a similar raid. The Yankee soldiers, though, were far from distressed by Dow's capture. They were dissatisfied with the leadership of their generals at the siege, and actually thought that one less general around would be to their advantage. As Sergeant Lawrence Van Alstyne of the 128th New York put it, "I'll bet if every officer in Banks' army, and General Banks with them, was tied up in a bag and dumped in the river, the privates could take Port Hudson in the next twenty-four hours."

Entrenchments occupied by the Confederates during Banks' siege.

With the capitulation of Vicksburg, Port Hudson surrendered as well.

Old Glory finally flies over the Confederate works at Port Hudson.

In late June Gardner received the sad news that General Johnston would be unable to advance to his relief from Jackson. Consequently he had no choice but to hold on as long as his food and ammunition held out. Banks, on the other hand, was under pressure of a different kind. It seems that Confederate General Dick Taylor had led his small army of 4500 towards New Orleans and was severely threatening Banks' lines of supply and communications. Banks had campaigned seriously against Taylor earlier in the year, but never had been able to bring the able rebel to bay. Now that Banks was tied up with most of his troops at Port Hudson, Taylor took advantage of the situation to advance on New Orleans, which was only held by a small garrison. Brigadier General William Emory, the commander at New Orleans, was soon warning Banks that a major crisis was developing in that front.

This news forced Banks to try another desperate assault to end the siege. In late June, two tunnels had been constructed under the Confederate works. On the far left, Engineer Captain Joseph Bailey built a long zigzag sap and then a tunnel under the Confederate fort at the Citadel. A longer tunnel was constructed under the direction of Engineer Captain Palfrey that had the Priest Cap as its goal. Banks decided to use Palfrey's sap and tunnel as a springboard to take the Priest Cap. He alerted his 1000-man Forlorn Hope and prepared an attack for the 4th of July.

Everyone in the Confederate lines was expecting an attack on the 4th. At the Priest Cap, Colonel Thomas H. Johnston of the 1st Mississippi noted suspicious enemy activity in the Union lines opposite his position. He had for several days suspected that the Yankees might be tunneling under his works, so he had unsuccessfully dug several short counter tunnels. On July 3 he decided to put some powder in one of his tunnels and set it off to see what would happen. The blast caused Palfrey's tunnel to collapse, and so indefinitely postponed Bank's assault.

Banks' attention now was focused on a second tunnel being constructed by Captain Bailey under the Citadel at the southern end of the Confederate defenses. When it was ready, he would try another attack.

But the attack never came off. On 7 July Banks received the following welcome message from Grant, dated 4 July: "The garrison of Vicksburg surrendered this morning." The news spread like wildfire, and the weary troops began cheering. The Confederates hollered over to see what was happening, and refused at first to believe the news. When General Gardner heard the news, he sent a note to ask Banks for verification and a truce. Gardner knew he only had a week's worth of food left, now that the mules and dogs were gone. Banks at first balked at a truce: so Gardner sent another note that stated "Having defended this position as long as I deem my duty requires, I am willing to surrender to you."

Terms of surrender were negotiated on 8 July: common soldiers would be paroled and sent home, officers would be sent to prison camps. Because the actual surrender proceedings were put off until 9 July, many Confederate officers took advantage of the delay to sneak off through the swamps on the night of the 8th. To receive the surrender, Banks staged a magnificent parade that included two picked regiments from each division, plus other select troops. In honor of Gardner's gallantry during the battle, Banks returned his sword to him after it was surrendered.

Altogether the Confederates surrendered 5500 men, 60 guns, 150,000 rounds of ammunition, and about 45,000 pounds of gunpowder. Gardner's combat losses during the siege totaled about 200 killed, 800 wounded, 200 died of disease, 150 captured, and 250 deserted. These brought the total Confederate losses to about 7100. Of the 5500 who surrendered on 9 July, about 500 were wounded and some 2000 were sick. Bank's admitted losses were 707 killed, 3336 wounded, and 319 missing, for a total of 4362. His actual losses were probably much higher. It should also be mentioned that these figures do not include those who died or were incapacitated by sickness.

Thus Port Hudson fell after a 44-day siege. In the end it was not captured due to any skill or assault by General Banks, but because of Vicksburg's surrender to Grant. This fact chagrined Banks for the rest of his life, even though he received the thanks of Congress for his "victory."

Union troops work to pin down the enemy during the attack.

General Grant himself, writing an article for *Century Magazine*, described what happened to the unlucky Confederates still posted where the mine exploded: "There were a few men, however, left at the advance line, and others working in the counter-mine. . . . All that were there were thrown up into the air, some of them coming down on our side, still alive. I remember one colored man, who had been underground at work, when the explosion took place, who was thrown to our side. He was not much hurt, but was terribly frightened. Someone asked him about how high he had gone up. 'Dunno, Massa, but tink 'bout t'ree mile,' was the reply. General Logan commanded at this point, and took the colored man to his quarters, where he did service to the end of the siege."

The blast of the mine was a signal for all the Union forces to open up all along the line. As they blazed away, an assault column rushed forward to seize the demolished Confederate fort. The attack was spearheaded by the 45th Illinois, supported by the remainder of Leggett's brigade. The troops had little difficulty entering the crater left by the blast. But once in it, they found difficulty climbing up its sides to get at the enemy, who had formed along their secondary line behind the Great Redoubt. The Illinois troops then had no choice but to form a defensive position along the rim of the crater. They kept firing until their gun barrels were too hot to touch. Then they began firing muskets loaded and passed forward by the troops in their rear.

Hand grenades were used abundantly by both sides in this fight. Here the Confederates held a distinct advantage. The grenades they tossed into the bomb crater rolled to its center, where their blast scattered fragments throughout the crater's bowl. The Confederates also managed to train a nearby cannon directly on the crater, which they fired on with great effect.

The Union commanders decided that there would be no great advantage to continue assaulting the new Confederate line behind the captured redoubt. Instead of attacking more, General Leggett directed his men to consolidate their position in the cratered ruin of the Great Redoubt. Meanwhile the Confederates were having all they could do to hold onto their position. The 3rd Louisiana, already partially shattered by the mine blast, was extremely hard pressed. It was soon reinforced by the 6th Missouri of Bowen's division. The commander of the 6th, Colonel Erwin, was a grandson of the noted orator and politician, Henry Clay. Erwin was killed while leading his men into position shouting "Come on my brave boys, don't let the Third Regiment ahead of you!"

Federal troops desperately attempt to exploit the gap made by the mine.

The 45th Illinois charges into the crater created by the mine explosion under Fort Hill.

The vicious fight in the crater as the Yankees drive once more into the breach defended by members of the 3rd Louisiana and 6th Mississippi.

Fraternizing With The Foe

In a war like the Civil War, where most of the soldiers of each side shared a common language, history, culture and traditions, it was not strange for the soldiers of blue and gray to drop their guard and fraternize with each other when occasion permitted. This occurred most often when the opposing sides held one position for a long time, such as in sieges or long encampments. Stories abound of pickets declaring temporary cease-fires when they could; they figured such temporary interruptions would not affect the course of the war.

Besides conversing regularly with each other, opposing pickets even conducted bartering sessions—Yankee newspapers, salt or coffee would be exchanged for Southern tobacco or honey. This trading took place face to face, or sometimes dogs were used. Along the Rappahannock River in Central Virginia, opposing pickets exchanged trade goods by miniature boats. In early 1863 some New Jersey troops near Fredericksburg received the following note from a Mississippi private:

"Gents: U.S. Army. We send you some tobacco by our packet. Send us some coffee in return. Also a deck of cards if you have them, and we will send you more tobacco. Send us any late papers if you have them."

Similar fraternization occurred at more than one location because of the closeness of the opposing lines during the 47 days' siege of Vicksburg. Sometimes the Confederate troops taunted the Yankees for their lack of success and asked them when they were going to come into town for a visit. The Yankees replied that they would come visiting when the Rebels showed their better manners; besides, Pemberton's men were so well hemmed in they weren't going to do any sight-seeing of their own. Then the Yankees would ask how well the Confederates were enjoying their mule and dog meat. So the exchanges would go back and forth.

At one point during the siege such fraternization led to a friendship being formed between William Duffner of the 24th Indiana of Hovey's Division, 13th Corps, and a Confederate named A.K. Shaifer. For some reason Duffner made a wooden rocking chair during the siege, and after Vicksburg's fall gave it to his friend with the inscription "From William Duffner, Yank, to A.K. Shaifer, Reb; may God forgive, unite and bless us all." This unusual war relic is preserved today in a museum in Grand Gulf, Mississippi.

Coonskin's tower stands over the vacated trenches at Vicksburg after the town's surrender.

As soon as Leggett consolidated his new position, he set his men to work constructing yet another mine. In addition, he expanded and widened the approach saps so that he could get more men up to the front lines. The new mine was completed and exploded on 1 July, demolishing another Confederate redan. However, Grant ordered no attack made to follow up this second explosion. He had learned his lesson on the 25th, that there was no great advantage to be gained by such an assault. Nevertheless, mining and counter-mining continued right up until the time that Vicksburg surrendered on 4 July. The surrender canceled the detonation of a third mine explosion scheduled for 6 July.

Thus the Vicksburg mine exploded on the 25th was more notable for its construction and expectations than for any military advantage it gained. Given the length of the siege and the suitable terrain for a mine, it was only natural for the Yankees to make the attempt, and, despite its lack of material success and all the work that went into it, there was no one who really regretted having made the attempt.

Vicksburg was not the only battle where underground mines were dug and exploded. By far the largest and most famous mine assault was one set off at Petersburg, Virginia, on 30 July 1864. This mine, constructed by coal miners in the 48th Pennsylvania, was a complex 511 feet long. It was charged with 8,000 pounds of gun powder, almost four times as much as the 25 June Vicksburg mine. The mine's explosion obliterated nine companies of Confederate troops and created a crater 170 feet long, 80 feet wide and 30 feet deep, several times larger than the Vicksburg mine. As had happened at Vicksburg, the attacking Union troops easily reached the mine crater but had difficulty passing beyond it. Large bodies of troops had been assigned to follow up the initial charge into the crater, but they were not used properly. Thus the Petersburg mine and the ensuing Battle of the Crater turned out to be a stupendous failure, as U.S. Grant succinctly put it. One would think he would have learned more from the lesson presented by the great mine at Vicksburg.

Night falls as the fray in the crater continues. Finding they could press on no further, the Federals sought some consolation in the gains made by possible by the explosion of the mine.

Soldiers embroiled in the fight use grenades to advance their positions.

CHAPTER XI

THE SURRENDER

As the siege progressed, Grant received a steady stream of reinforcements from his own department and departments farther afield. His most immediate source was his own 16th Corps, which was guarding the railroads from Memphis to Corinth. As already mentioned, Lauman's division of this corps arrived on 28 May and was used to extend the siege lines from McClernand's left toward the river. This line was completed when Herron's division from the Department of Missouri came up on 8 June. Kimball's newly formed division of the 16th Corps reached Grant on 3 June and was used to guard the district north of Vicksburg at Haynes' Bluff. He was reinforced there on 11 June by W.S. Smith's division of the 16th corps, and by Parke's 9th Corps from the Department of Ohio, which arrived on June 14.

The arrival of all these reinforcements raised Grant's strength from 50,000 at the end of May to 77,000 in mid-June. This enabled him to split his command in two, half to continue the siege of Vicksburg and the other half to keep an eye on Johnston's growing army at Jackson. Grant assigned command of this new force to his trusted lieutenant, William T. Sherman. Sherman's command consisted of Parke's 9th Corps and other troops already at or near Haynes' Bluff, a total of 34,000 men. With these he was

Pemberton's works at Vicksburg. The Confederate's held on for as long as possible with soldiers and civilians suffering from severe tribulations. However, by early July, Pemberton was finally forced to bow to the inevitable and surrendered.

responsible for a line from Haynes' Bluff to the Vicksburg and Jackson railroad bridge over the Big Black River.

Throughout the siege, Grant had more than just Johnston's force at Jackson to worry about in his rear. Banks was keeping Gardner closed in at Port Hudson, but there were no forces assigned to block General Kirby Smith's trans-Mississippi army. Authorities in Richmond for a long time were urging Smith to do something to help Port Hudson or Vicksburg. Finally Smith in late May directed Major General Dick Taylor to take his 3,000 men and try to relieve Vicksburg. Taylor felt such an expedition would be folly, since it was impossible for him to cross the Mississippi from Louisiana in order to reach Vicksburg. He thought it would be much better for his force to try to help Gardner at Port Hudson. Nevertheless, he obeyed his orders and made an attack on 7 June against Grant's garrisons at Young's Point and Miliken's Bend. All he managed to do was chase the Yankees into their defenses before he was forced to retreat. When Taylor heard that Kirby Smith had recalled a 4,000-man division sent to reinforce him, he withdrew from the Vicksburg area to the district west of Baton Rouge, where he would threaten New Orleans and Banks' supply lines.

Taylor's brief incursion was but a minor annoyance to Grant compared to the size of Johnston's army, which grew to over 31,000 by the end of June. As already explained, Johnston at the battle of Jackson on 14 May had only 6,000 men, composed of Gist's brigade from the South Carolina defenses, Maxey's brigade from Port Hudson, and Gregg's and Walker's brigades. After the loss of Jackson, Johnston moved north to Canton. Here he was reinforced on 20 May by two brigades (Ector's and McNair's) from Chattanooga. In the next few days he was joined by Maxey's brigade from the Port Hudson garrison and Loring's division, which had become separated from Pemberton's army after the battle of Champion's Hill on 16 May. By 3 June he received even more reinforcements: Evans' brigade from South Carolina, and two divisions from Bragg's army at Chattanooga, John C. Breckinridge's infantry division and W.H. Jackson's cavalry division.

Johnston was an excellent defensive general, but was not the right man to take aggressive charge of the complicated situation posed by Grant's crossing of the Mississippi on 27 April. His attempts to get Pemberton to join him north of Jackson on 15 and 16 May led directly to Pemberton's defeat at Champion's Hill. Johnston then did not see the sense in defending Vicksburg if it meant losing Pemberton's army, but was not able to assert his authority as Pemberton's superior enough to get Pemberton to abandon his fortress.

After the siege began, Johnston stayed in Grant's rear at Canton waiting for the right opportunity to come to Pemberton's aid. The problem was that the longer he waited, the stronger Grant's army became. This situation discouraged him, as he looked more and more to aid from Kirby Smith rather than forcing an issue with his own army, which was really Vicksburg's best hope. Pemberton understood this, as did all the defenders of Vicksburg, but he could not get Johnston to advance despite his desperate messages citing his low ammunition and dwindling food supply. Johnston kept replying to Richmond and to Pemberton that he simply did not have enough men, enough transport, enough supplies.

Johnston at length ordered his advance on 28 June. His troops did not really get under way until 1 July. On 2 July he reached the Big Black River with three of his divisions, and came upon Sherman's defensive positions. In typical Johnston form, he now spent three days scouting Sherman's position prior to committing to a line of advance. He decided to advance by way of Edwards' Station, but it was now too late. Late on the 4th he heard of Pemberton's surrender. He had no choice now but to turn back to Jackson.

In the middle of June, Pemberton came to realize that his position was becoming desper-

Pemberton seeks terms from U.S. Grant. Originally, Grant only offered unconditional surrender, but, later, granted more generous terms.

ate. The Union siege of lines were within 100 yards of his works, often less, and Grant's engineers were probably preparing to set off more mines like the one that went off on 25 June. One-third of his men were on the sick list, leaving only 15,000 fit for duty, a number greatly outnumbered by Grant's command. Everyone was suffering from reduced rations, which would soon run out entirely. Some of his men were already reduced to eating mule meat, which was being issued to those who would eat it. Reportedly it was not too bad, and tasted as good as venison. The citizens of Vicksburg were buying up all the mule meat they could get at $1 a pound. Others were reduced to eating rats or "other small deer."

Pemberton's one great hope was to hold on until Johnston could come to his relief. On 12 June he wrote his superior, "I am waiting most anxiously to know your intentions. . . . I shall endeavor to hold out as long as we have anything to eat." His determination was severely undercut by a message from Johnston received two days later but dated 29 May: "I am too weak to save Vicksburg. Can do no more than attempt to save you and your garrison. It will be impossible to extricate you unless you cooperate and we make mutually supporting movements. Communicate your plans and suggestions if possible."

Pemberton knew too well that his force was too weak to cut its way out through Grant's siege lines, so he never responded to Johnston's requests for his plans. Instead, he wrote the following to Johnston on 20 June, during one of the greatest artillery bombardments of the siege: "I hope you will advance with the least possible delay. My men have been thirty-four days in trenches without relief, and the enemy within conversation distance. We are living on very reduced rations, and, as you know, are entirely isolated. What aid am I to expect from you?"

Federal troops arriving in the vicinity of Vicksburg to join Grant. With the Federals receiving massive reinforcements and supplies, any hope for the relief of Vicksburg dimmed.

Citizens' Life in Vicksburg during the Siege

The 5000 citizens of Vicksburg were relatively unaffected by the first year of the war because of the security offered by the defenses of New Orleans downstream and the Tennessee armies upstream. The first real threat of war did not come until 27 April 1862, when the sad news came that New Orleans had fallen. Vicksburg's citizens knew well that this meant Yankee armies would soon be at their doorstep. Immediately merchants began packing up their goods for transfer to less threatened points, and light manufacturers and artisans moved what machinery they could. Plantation owners prepared to burn their cotton stores as soon as the Yankees arrived, and many families moved out of town to weather the storm with friends or country cousins. The citizens who remained were ready to fight to the end rather than surrender their city. Some were even prepared to burn it rather than see it fall into enemy hands.

The city first came under fire on the afternoon of 27 May, when Union gunboats that had come up the river from New Orleans opened up a barrage. Provident residents at once sought refuge in their basements. A few curious onlookers who went to see the Union warships were sent scurrying for cover as soon as the bombardment opened. As soon as the firing stopped, many families chose to head for the country. Patriotism was one thing, but enemy shells and the noise of combat was quite another. One Vicksburg family packed up and headed for an abandoned plantation they knew ten miles outside of town. When they got there, they found four other families already moved in.

The great cannonade that began when Admiral Farragut ran his fleet past Vicksburg's batteries early on 28 June drove still more citizens to seek shelter in the country. Many headed east of town, away from the Yankee boats and their deadly guns. One resident did not make it. Mrs. Alice Gamble was hit by a shell and died a few minutes later, the first of a number of Vicksburg civilians to die during the fighting.

When the Union fleets finally sailed away, defeated, in July, some residents returned to the city in an attempt to restore normalcy. They found their houses slightly damaged, but still standing. Dust, mud, and soldiers were everywhere. The worst thing was probably the shortages in clothing and food occasioned by the presence of so many soldiers in town. This, however, did not deter soldiers and civilians from having a grand ball on Christmas Eve. The town put on much less of a spectacle when President Jefferson Davis passed through town during a military inspection tour in mid December.

Things seemed so peaceful in Vicksburg in the spring of 1863 that the citizens planned a grand ball for the night of 16 April. Many who had been in temporary exile outside of town returned for the occasion, and were surprised to find shell holes in almost every house. The ball began as scheduled, despite the ominous presence of newly arrived Yankee warships in the river. Then all became mayhem as Admiral Porter, who had heard of the ball, used the occasion to run his fleet past the city's river batteries. When the batteries of both sides opened up, the party broke up, with the soldiers heading for their units and the civilians heading for shelter. More than one Southern belle saw her dress ruined when she had to dive to the ground for cover as she ran home that night.

The citizens of Vicksburg had a sense of something terribly wrong when they learned of the battle of Champion Hill on 16 May. Soon weary, dejected soldiers began to file into the town's defenses. The scene made a lasting impression on Dora Miller: "I shall never forget the woeful sight of a beaten, demoralized army that came rushing back - humanity in the throes of endurance. Worn, hollow-eyed, ragged, footsore, bloody, the men limped along unarmed, but followed by siege guns, ambulances, gun carriages, and wagons in aimless confusion. At twilight two or three bands on the court-house hill and other points began playing Dixie, Bonnie Blue Flag, and so on, and the drums began to beat all about; I suppose they were rallying the scattered army."

Besides the arriving army, Vicksburg was also filled with hordes of refugees driven before the advancing Yankees like gulls before a storm. Ironically, many of these refugees were the same residents of Vicksburg who had gone to country plantations in order to escape the fighting along the Mississippi. Now they had to undergo two perils, first trying to escape Grant's advancing army, and then having to endure the siege.

As soon as the siege began, most of the civilians in Vicksburg realized they were not safe even in the basements of their houses because of the constant shellfire and danger from fires. Those who could sought shelter in caves that were hollowed out of the soft soil in Vicksburg's numerous hillsides. Caves were made in all shapes and sizes, some so large that they held numerous families and as many as 200 people. Cave life soon developed its own rules and routine, much as life in the subways of London during the air raids of World War II.

Caves were hollowed out to be the size of a room in a regular house. As occupants spent more time there, they made additional rooms connected by corridors. Closets and shelves were built into the cave walls, and floors were covered with planks. The biggest complaint about the caves was their dampness. Often carpets or other hangings were draped on the walls to conceal the dampness somewhat. Some families used the caves only as bombshelters and slept whenever they could on porches or in nearby tents. Lida Lord had one of the fancier caves around: "The cave ran about twenty feet underground and communicated at right angles with a wing which opened on the front of the hill, giving us a free circulation fair. At the door was an arbor of branches, in which, on a pine table, we dined when shelling permitted. Near it were a dug-out fireplace and an open-air kitchen, with table, pans, etc."

Caves became prime pieces of real estate as the siege dragged on. Enterprising Negro laborers would dig them out at $30-$50 each, while cave "realtors" might sell them or lease them for $15 a month. At first most of the caves were built facing east so as to avoid the fire of the gunboats in the river. However, as the siege went on, heavy fire also came from the landward batteries, forcing everyone to be vigilant. Everyone, even the children, developed quick reactions each time a bombardment started; they would drop everything and head for shelter, just like civilians did during the air raids of World War II. Lida Lord wrote: "It was curious to see how well trained the little ones were. At night, when the bombs began to fly like pigeons over our heads, they would be waked out of a sound sleep, would slip on their shoes, and run, without a word, like rabbits to their burrows. In the daytime they climbed the trees, gathered papaws, and sometimes went blackberrying up the road, but never far, for the first sound of cannonading sent them scampering home."

There is no question that Vicksburg during the siege was a dangerous place for civilians, whether they lived in town or in the caves. Obviously, the houses were a much more hazardous place to be. One young mother refused to leave her home on Adams Street because her four month old son was sick. She saw a shell enter the baby's bedroom and knock the child dead against the wall. But the caves were also dangerous. Lida Lord saw a woman's baby killed at her breast. Another woman rushed to grab her child when a barrage began, and had her arm severed by a shell. Lida saw her own brother stop to pick something up and almost get cut in two by a shell that scorched his back as it whizzed by.

Some citizens who did not like the caves instead sought shelter in Vicksburg's churches. It was claimed that church benches made quite good beds. The Yankee attackers at least had the civility not to aim directly at the churches, or at the hospitals, and these were struck only occasionally by stray shells.

In addition to the constant danger posed by enemy shells, the citizens of Vicksburg were hard pressed by hunger and the shortage of good water. Finding potable water was a constant problem, since there was a limited number of wells and cisterns and the muddy river water could not be used. Food sources were more available, but in limited supplies, especially after the soldiers went on half rations of 140 ounces of food a piece per day. Basic foods could be obtained from the merchants in town even at the height of the siege, but for exorbitant prices. Flour was $200 a barrel, sugar $30 a barrel, corn $100 a bushel and bacon $5 a pound. Coffee could not be obtained for any price, so various substitutions were tried, such as sweet potato coffee. Some citizens grew so enraged at the profiteering of the town merchants that they set fire to a row of shops on the evening of 2 June.

The pressure of poor food and the constant threat of death made Dora Miller quite tense and unhappy: "The cellar is so damp and musty the bedding has to be carried out and laid in the sun everyday, with the forecast that it may be demolished at any moment. The confinement is dreadful. To sit and listen as if waiting for death in a horrible manner would drive me insane . . . I am so tired of corn bread, which I never liked, that I eat it with tears in my eyes. We are lucky to get a quart of milk daily from a family near who have a cow they hourly expect to be killed. I send five dollars to market each morning, and it buys a small piece of mule meat. Rice and milk is my main food; I can't eat the mule meat. We boil the rice and eat it cold with milk for supper. Martha runs the gauntlet to buy the meat and milk once a day in perfect terror."

J.M. Swords, editor of Vicksburg's newspaper the *Daily Citizen*, attempted to keep up the morale of both soldiers and citizens by writing editorials encouraging good spirits and condemning the profiteers. When the *Daily Whig* was burned down by a direct shell hit on 9 May, Swords' paper was Vicksburg's only remaining periodical. Keeping it in business proved to be a hard job. On 16 June his office was hit by a mortar shell that came through the roof and fell straight into the basement. It made a big mess, but did not harm the presses. Swords had more of a problem when he began to run out of newsprint. He found a good substitute by using the back side of wallpaper rolls. Some Vicksburg citizens thus got a bonus when they bought the *Daily Citizen*. After reading the news, they could paste the wallpaper to the wall and enjoy its pink and green flowered design.

Swords' last issue of the *Daily Citizen* was published on wallpaper on 2 July. It contained good news about Lee's invasion of Pennsylvania and Port Hudson's heroic defense against Banks' army. Swords could not bring himself to prepare an edition on 3 July after surrender negotiations were begun. When Union troops entered town on 4 July, they came to his shop and found the type still set for the 2 July issue. A few knowledgeable soldiers started up the presses again to reprint the 2 July edition, with the following paragraph added: "Note: July 4th 1863. Two days bring about great changes. The banner of the Union floats over Vicksburg. General Grant has 'caught the rabbit'; he has dined in Vicksburg, and he did bring his dinner with him. The *Citizen* lives to see it. For the last time it appears on 'wall-paper'. No more will it eulogize the luxury of mule meat and fricasseed kitten—urge Southern warriors to such diet nevermore. This is the last wall-paper edition, and is, excepting this note, from the types we found them. It will be valuable hereafter as a curiosity."

The victor meets with the vanquished: Grant visits with Pemberton after the Confederate surrender.

Pemberton sent this message via his most reliable courier, a Captain George D. Wise. Wise somehow made it through to Johnston, but was captured on the return trip while carrying Johnston's reply. Two later messages, though, did make it through. Both urged Pemberton to try to escape with his men, either by fighting his way out along the Jackson Road or by swimming across the river.

Pemberton was especially concerned for the suffering of his men in the trenches. He must have been deeply affected by an anonymous Appeal for Help dated 28 June; the contents of the letter were not made public until years after the war. After praising Pemberton and the army's performance, the letter got down to hard facts: "Our rations have been cut down to 1 biscuit, and a small bit of bacon per day, not enough scarcely to keep soul and body together, much less stand the hardships we are called upon to stand. . . . We are and have been kept close in the trenches day and night, not allowed to forage at all and even if permitted there is nothing to be had among the citizens. Men don't want to starve and don't intend to, but they call upon you for justice. . . . If you can't feed us, you had better surrender us, horrible as the idea is, than suffer this noble army to disgrace themselves by desertion. . . . The army is now ripe for mutiny unless it can be fed. . . . "

Feeling that the end was near, Pemberton asked his four division commanders what condition their troops were in and whether they were able to march and fight their way out in an "evacuation." Three of the generals responded that the men had good spirits and could continue to hold their lines, but they lacked the strength to mount an attack. Only Stevenson felt his men would rather fight their way out than be captured.

Rather than risk continued fruitless loss of life, Pemberton penned the following note to Grant:

"General: I have the honor to propose to you an armistice for several hours, with a view to arranging terms for the capitulation of Vicksburg. To this end, if agreeable to you, I will appoint three commissioners to meet a like number, to be named by yourself, at such place and hour today as you may find convenient. I make this proposition to save the further effusion of blood, which must otherwise be shed to a frightful extent, feeling myself fully able to

maintain my position for a yet indefinite period."

Grant was in no mood to discuss anything but unconditional surrender, as his blunt reply states:

"The useless profusion of blood you propose stopping by this course can be ended at any time you choose, by the unconditional surrender of the city and garrison. Men who have shown so much endurance and courage as those now in Vicksburg will always challenge the respect of an adversary, and I can assure you that you will be treated with all the respect due to prisoners of war."

At 1500 that afternoon the two top generals met at an old oak tree between the lines. Generals Bowen and Montgomery accompanied Pemberton, while Grant had with him Generals Ord, McPherson, Logan, and A.J. Smith; Sherman was absent facing Johnston's army. The meeting did not go well, and broke up without terms being agreed on. Grant left stating he would send his terms that night, and Pemberton could take them or leave them.

Grant's final terms presented that night were more generous than his "unconditional surrender" hard line. He would allow officers to keep their side arms and personal property, as well as one horse if they had one. Most importantly, he would parole all Pemberton's men rather than send them to prison camps. The surrender would take place at 0800 the next morning when Grant would send one division into Vicksburg to begin making paroles. Pemberton realized these were more generous terms than he expected, so he accepted them, even though it would mean the humiliation of surrendering on the Fourth of July. Delaying negotiations, he thought, would only bring about harsher terms. The sole change he requested in the surrender terms was for the defenders to march out of their works at 1000 and lay down their arms. This simple act would allow them to surrender themselves, but not their fortress. Grant could then send troops in to occupy the city. Quite to Pemberton's surprise, Grant accepted the change.

The surrender came off as scheduled. Pemberton had only 11,000 healthy men able to participate. They marched out of their works with their flags flying and their heads held high. The Union troops stood by in silent respect. After laying down their arms, most of the Confederates wept to see the Union flag flying atop their works and at the courthouse in the center of town. As diarist Willie Turnnard observed, "It was a sad spectacle for the ragged, emaciated, yet heroic Confederates, who had so stubbornly endeavored to retain possession of this stronghold."

With the enemy batteries on the Vicksburg bluffs finally silenced, the Federal gunboat Choctaw rests before the capitulated city.

The starved citizens of Vicksburg watch as the triumphant soldiers of Grant's army enter the Confederate citadel on the Mississippi.

EPILOGUE

General Johnston was preparing to move against Grant's rear on 4 July when he received the sad news that Vicksburg had surrendered. He promptly ordered a retreat to Jackson, which he reached on the 7th. Here he posted his 36,000 men in the line of rifle pits erected earlier under Pemberton's orders. The line was not a particularly strong one, stretching in a westward arc from the Canton Road northwest of town to the Pearl River south of town. Johnston posted Loring's division on the right of his line, Walker and French in the center, and Breckinridge on the left, with cavalry on both flanks.

Johnston's command was pursued by Sherman, who had been guarding Grant's rear from the Big Black River railroad bridge to Haynes' Bluff. Sherman had a makeshift force of 48,000 men, consisting of the 9th Corps, 13th Corps, 15th Corps, one division of the 16th Corps and one division of the 17th Corps. Altogether he had twelve divisions under his command, comprising two-thirds of Grant's army.

Sherman's advance forces reached the outskirts of Jackson on the night of 9 July and began skirmishing with Johnston's outposts. He closed in on the city the next day, placing the 9th Corps on the left, 15th in the center and 13th on the right. Sherman felt the enemy lines were too strong to attack head on, so he prepared for a siege, figuring that Johnston did not have enough supplies stored up to hold on for long.

Sharp skirmishing began on the 10th and lasted for several days. Sherman was still in no hurry to direct an assault, though a division of the 13th Corps became more heavily engaged than ordered during a reconnaissance on 12 July. Johnston was in no shape to withstand a siege, and was disappointed when Sherman did not press forward any assaults. The Confederates withdrew across the Pearl River on the night of 16 July, and retreated to the northwest. The next day Sherman followed for about 12 miles before calling it quits and returning to Vicksburg. During the brief campaign Sherman lost about 1,100 men and Johnston 1,300, over half of them prisoners.

Young Southerners who served in Confederate ranks. The fall of Vicksburg was one of two blows inflicted on the hopes of the Confederacy on 4 July 1863. The other was Lee's retreat from Gettysburg.

Bibliography

By far the greatest living expert on the Vicksburg Campaign is Edwin C. Bearss, chief historian of the National Park Service and longtime historian at the Vicksburg National Military Park. His mammoth three-volume study *The Campaign for Vicksburg* (Dayton, Ohio, 1985-1986) is by far the most detailed account of the battle and siege. These volumes, however, study only Grant's several campaigns against the city and do not cover the interesting 1862 naval expeditions. It should also be noted that Bearss' style is a bit dry and analytical.

Bearss is also the author of several other monographs dealing with the campaign. His *Decision in Mississippi* (Jackson, 1962) covers all the wartime activity in the state, including the battles of Iuka and Corinth and other actions not covered in *The Campaign for Vicksburg*. Bearss was responsible for the salvaging of the USS *Cairo*, and wrote *Hardluck Ironclad, The Sinking and Salvage of the Cairo* in 1966. Yet another campaign story by him is *The Battle of Jackson, the Siege of Jackson, and Three Other Post-Vicksburg Actions* (Baltimore, 1981).

There are numerous recent narrative accounts of the Vicksburg campaign that give a good overview supplemented with anecdotes and human interest stories. The best of these are: *The Final Fortress, The Campaign for Vicksburg, 1862-1863*, by Samuel Carter III (New York, 1980); *The Web of Victory, Grant at Vicksburg*, by Earl S. Miers (New York, 1955); *Vicksburg*, by A.A. Hoehling (Englewood Cliffs, 1969); and *Grant Moves South* by Bruce Catton (New York, 1960).

Just about everything you would want to know about the siege of Port Hudson can be found in David C. Edwards' thorough two- volume study, *The Guns of Port Hudson* (Lafayette, Louisiana, 1983 and 1984). There is a good short account of the campaign by Richard B. Irwin in volume 3 of *Battles and Leaders of the Civil War* (New York, 1889). Other background material can be found in *The Civil War in Louisiana* by John D. Winters (Baton Rouge, 1963).

Several of the highest ranking generals in the campaign wrote autobiographies covering their war records. Most notable of these is Grant's *Personal Memoirs of U.S. Grant* (New York, 1885), which has been acclaimed as one of the best military autobiographies ever written. Sherman's *Memoirs of General William T. Sherman* (New York, 1875) is good but less detailed on the Vicksburg campaign. Admiral David D. Porter described his often frustrating experiences in the campaign in his naval *History of the Civil War* (New York, 1886). The Confederate view of the campaign can be read in Joseph E. Johnston's *Narrative of Military Operations Directed During the Late War Between the States* by Joseph E. Johnston (New York, 1874).

Battles and Leaders of the Civil War (New York, 1989, with several later reprints) contains a variety of good first-hand accounts of the Vicksburg campaign by major figures such as Grant, Johnston and Pemberton. Also included are articles by important lesser known figures including S.M. Lockett (the chief Confederate engineer at the siege), Isaac X. Brown (commander of the gunboat *Arkansas*), and Andrew Hickenlooper. Individual battle accounts from the army commanders down to captains of batteries have been published, along with their messages and telegrams, in *War of the Rebellion, The Official Records of the Union and Confederate Armies* (Washington, 1880-1891). Reports concerning Vicksburg are in Volume 24 (three parts), and Port Hudson is covered in Volume 26 (2 parts).

The events of the siege made a deep impression on the soldiers who served in the trenches at Vicksburg. One of the most detailed Southern diaries of the siege is Willie H. Tunnard's *A Southern Record, The Story of the Third Louisiana Infantry CSA* (1866, reprinted 1988). The following two Union personal accounts came highly recommended: *A Soldier's Story of the Siege of Vicksburg* by Osborn M. Oldroyd (Springfield, Ill., 1885), and William W. Orme's *Civil War Letters* (1930). Northern reporter Sylvanus Cadwallader wrote his impressions of the campaign in *Three Years with General Grant* (New York, 1955). Lastly, a mention should be made of the experiences of the Englishman Lt. Colonel Arthur L. Freemantle during the early stages of the siege, as recorded in his *The Freemantle Diary* (New York, 1954).

The suffering of the civilians during the Vicksburg siege has been recorded most memorably by Mary A. Loughborough in *My Cave Life at Vicksburg* (New York, 1864). Other eyewitness accounts of the siege are collected in Richard Wheeler's *The Siege of Vicksburg* (New York, 1978).

There have been a number of biographies written of the two principal Union commanders during the campaign. All earlier studies of U.S. Grant have been eclipsed by William S. McFeely's recent *Grant, A Biography* (New York, 1981). Nothing as authoritative has recently been written of Sherman. Best of the older biographies are: *Sherman, Fighting Prophet*, by Lloyd Lewis (New York, 1932); *William Tecumseh Sherman*, by James M. Merrill (New York, 1971); and *Merchant of Terror, General Sherman and Total War*, by John B. Walters (New York, 1973). For Grant's lesser lieutenants, *Grant and His Generals* by Clarence MacArthey (New York, 1953) can be recommended. It contains chapters on Generals Logan, McPherson and McClernand, as well as Sherman.

Many fewer biographies have been written on the principal Confederate leaders in the campaign. A balanced study of J.E. Johnston is given in *A Different Valor* by Gilbert E. Govan and James W. Livingwood (New York, 1956). *Pemberton, Defender of Vicksburg* by the General's grandson, John C. Pemberton (Chapel Hill, 1942) tries to be objective but cannot help being apologetic. *First With the Most*, Forrest by Robert S. Henry (1899, reprinted 1987) is perhaps the best of several biographies of the noted cavalry commander.

The exciting war on the Mississippi River from New Orleans and Memphis to Vicksburg has been studied in a wide variety of sources. The most comprehensive of these is perhaps *The Civil War at Sea, Volume 2: The River War* by Virgil Carrington Jones (New York, 1961). Also recommended are Civil War on Western Waters by Fletcher Pratt (New York, 1956), and *Guns on the Western Waters* by M.A. Gosnell (Baton Rouge, 1949). A good older account is *The Gulf and Inland Waters* by A.T. Mahan (New York, 1883).

Excellent first person accounts of the naval campaign, including a narrative by Admiral Porter on the taking of New Orleans, can be found in *Battles and Leaders of the Civil War*, volumes 2 and 3 (New York, 1889, with several recent reprints). *Damn the Torpedoes* is a good survey of the life of Admiral Farragut (New York, 1970). Good shorter biographies of Farragut, Porter and Foote can be found in *Mr. Lincoln's Admirals* by Clarence E. Macartney (New York, 1956).

By far the best study of each individual ship involved in the campaign is the recent book by Tony Gibbons entitled *Warships and Naval Battles of the Civil War* (New York, 1989). Younger readers will enjoy *Ironclads of the Civil War* by Frank R. Donovan and *American Heritage Magazine* (New York, 1964). The story of the USS *Cairo* is told in detail by her salvager, Edwin C. Bearss, in *Hardluck Ironclad, the Sinking and Salvage of the Cairo* (Baton Rouge, 1966).

Four books can be recommended on the role of cavalry actions during the Vicksburg campaign. *The Last Cavaliers* by Samuel Carter III (New York 1979) discusses the use of cavalry in general during the War. The use of Union cavalry in the campaign is covered in Volume 3 of *The Union Cavalry in the Civil War* by Stephen Z. Starr (Baton Rouge, 1985). *Grierson's Raid* by D. Alexander Brown (1954, reprint 1981) is probably the best individual study written on such an action in the War. This raid and Van Dorn's December 1862 attack on Holly Springs are both studied in *Mounted Raids of the Civil War* by Edward G. Langacre (Cranbury, New Jersey, 1975).

There are no specific studies available on the use of artillery in the Vicksburg campaign. However, two general reference books on the subject are useful: *Artillery and Ammunition Weapons of the Civil War* by Warren Ripley (New York, 1970), and *Field Artillery Weapons of the Civil War* by Hazlett, Olmstead, and Parks (Cranberry, New Jersey, 1983).

Small arms weapons and equipment used by the troops of both sides can be studied in Francis A. Lord's several volume *Civil War Collector's Encyclopedia* (first volume New York, 1973). Also recommended is Lord's *They Fought for the Union, A Complete Reference Work on the Federal Fighting Man* (New York, 1960). Younger and older readers alike will enjoy *Arms and Equipment of the Civil War* by Jack Coggins (New York, 1962).

The daily life of soldiers of both sides has been summarized in two recent books, *Civil War Soldiers, Their Expectations and Experiences* by Reid Mitchell (New York, 1988) and *Soldiers Blue and Gray* by James I. Robertson, Jr. (Columbia, South Carolina, 1988). These do not totally supplant two excellent older studies by Bell I. Wiley, *The Life of Billy Yank* (Indianapolis, 1951) and *The Life of Johhny Reb* (New York, 1971).

For general reference sources, the following books are recommended: *The Civil War Dictionary* by Mark M. Boatner III New York, 1959); *Historical Times Illustrated Encyclopedia of the Civil War*, edited by Patricia L. Faust (New York, 1986); and two biographical studies by Ezva Warner, *Generals in Gray* (Baton Rouge, 1959) and *Generals in Blue* (Baton Rouge, 1964).

Grant's Memoirs

General U.S. Grant's memoirs form a remarkable book, both for their content and for the conditions under which they were written. Following a generally unsuccessful two terms as president (1869-1877), Grant was bilked by his business partner, and found himself broke in 1884. Desperately needing money, he wrote three articles for $3000 for *Century Magazine's* Civil War series (now known as *Battles and Leaders of the Civil War*.) This contact led to an offer by *Century* for Grant to write two volumes of memoirs. Sam Clemens (Mark Twain), a friend of Grant's, heard of *Century's* offer and told him it was much too low. Clemens offered Grant a better deal to publish the memoirs with a publishing company he headed, the Charles L. Webster Company, and Grant agreed.

Right after he began writing, Grant found that he had throat cancer (perhaps he had smoked too many of the cigars that were his trademark). The work proceeded well for awhile, but then his health began to deteriorate. Nevertheless he continued on, writing in pencil on pads of lined paper. At times he could not write at all, or the morphine he took for pain left him so hazy he could not think straight. The general knew he was in a race against death. Yet he saw the fight as another war to be waged and won, just as he had overcome other conflicts in his roller coaster life.

Grant finished writing his memoirs less than a year after he started them. In his introduction, dated 1 July 1885, he stated, "The first volume, as well as a portion of the second, was written before I had reason to suppose I was in a critical condition of health. Later I was reduced almost to the point of death, and it became impossible for me to attend to anything for weeks. I have, however, somewhat regained my strength."

The general was well aware that he would not recover from his illness. Finishing his book had given him something to live for, and he indeed did triumph in this last battle. However, the constant writing also sapped his strength. Grant finished correcting his book proofs on 14 July 1885, and died on 23 July. His Herculean effort earned close to $500,000 for his family.

In writing his memoirs, Grant showed an unexpected clarity of style and purpose. The work is almost entirely military in scope. He speaks only briefly of his early life and says almost nothing of his postwar career. His recollections of the Mexican War constitute one of the best accounts available on that conflict. Likewise, he writes with a fine grasp of the totality of the Civil War. He seldom faults others unduly, though he is not always forthright about his own failures and weaknesses (for example, his drinking problems at Vicksburg). Grant had a firm grasp of the political side of the war, and strongly felt that the whole conflict was due to the slavery question. In an interesting postscript to the book, he spoke expertly of the international ramifications of the war, and even correctly predicted future racial tensions in the reunited United States.

Grant's book was received favorably in its time, and has gained in stature since then. Historians praise it for its clarity and objectivity, traits which enabled Grant to develop the strategy that won the war in 1863-1865. In addition, literary scholars praise the work for its forthrightness and pacing, and some even rank it with the writings of Caesar and Churchill as one of the world's greatest war memoirs.

Grant with his family a week before his death in 1885. 20 years earlier he was responsible for bringing a conclusion to the bloody war that gripped his nation.

Battlefield Parks

Vicksburg

Vicksburg National Military Park was created in 1899 under the auspices of the War Department. In 1933 it was transferred along with other battlefields to the jurisdiction of the National Park Service. Today it contains about 1800 acres of land located along the siege lines, running in a crescent for nine miles from Fort Hill north of Vicksburg to the bluffs south of town. Most of the park lands are in the northern and central parts of battle area; holdings in the southern part are limited to key points and connecting roadways. In a controversial move, the park in recent years has traded parcels on the southern portion of the field in order to consolidate its holdings farther north. Since the park completely embraces Vicksburg on its eastern (landward) side, there has been constant pressure on the park from civic development and other needs. The park is about equal in size to Antietam National Battlefield Site, and is about half the size of Shiloh or Gettysburg National Military Park.

The park includes about 30 miles of avenues, 130 cannons, 1600 markers, monuments and tablets, and 17 state memorials. Fortified lines are clearly marked and their defending units identified. Remains of forts and trenches are clearly visible, though visitors are not permitted to enter them all due to erosion problems. The only wartime building still standing within the park is the Shirley House, located opposite the Great Redoubt near the Jackson Road. The park has statues to Jefferson Davis and Generals Grant, Pemberton and Tilghman. Impressive state memorials have been erected by Mississippi, Louisiana, Arkansas, Missouri, Alabama, Michigan, Illinois, Wisconsin, Minnesota and Iowa.

The park museum is located near the center of the lines (at US 80). A second museum housing the USS *Cairo* and its artifacts is located near Fort Hill and the Vicksburg National Cemetery. The cemetery, established in 1866, contains the graves of about 17,000 Union soldiers, of whom some 13,000 are unknown.

Port Hudson

The battle at Port Hudson is remembered by the Port Hudson state commemorative area, administered by the state of Louisiana. This Park contains 643 acres located on the northern portion of the Confederate lines, in the area attacked by Weitzel on 27 May. Here there are six miles of trails, and elevated boardwalks above swampy areas. Some of the major forts along the river have eroded away, but there are still long stretches of original trenches to be seen. Union positions contained within the park include Fort Babcock and Artillery Ridge; Confederate works include Fort Desperate, Bennett's Redoubt, and Mississippi Redoubt. Unlike Vicksburg, Fort Hudson battlefield is not well marked, and has only a few cannons, markers and monuments.

The Port Hudson National Cemetery, containing some 3000 Union burials, is located in Slaughter's Field, where the New York Zouaves made their famous charge. The battlefield also has a small Confederate cemetery.

The town of Port Hudson no longer exists. After the war the Mississippi River changed course, leaving the Port Hudson docks land-locked. The town quickly withered away. Its inhabitants moved, and its buildings were dismantled or fell into ruins. Today only a few local plantation buildings are standing that date back to the time of the battle.

Grand Gulf

Grand Gulf Military Monument was created in 1962 to commemorate the battle of Port Gibson. It is located 10 miles northwest of the town of Port Gibson, and contains about 400 acres. Within the park are a small museum, the Grand Gulf Cemetery, Fort Cobun, Fort Wade, and some well preserved entrenchments.

Champion Hill

Champion Hill battlefield is still largely underdeveloped. It was declared a National Historic Landmark in 1977. Funds to preserve the battlefield are being sought by the Champion Hill Battlefield Foundation in Edwards, Mississippi.

Other Sites

Most other historical sites connected with the Vicksburg campaign contain only scattered and occasional commemorative markers. These include Bruinsburg, Fort Pemberton, Holly Springs, Jackson, Natchez and Raymond, Mississippi, Arkansas Post, Arkansas, and Hard Times, Lake Providence, Milliken's Bend, and New Carthage, Louisiana.